Climbing Higher
Unafraid

by Donna Martonfi

To Dawn and Sally:

How very blessed you are to have each other.

God Bless You Both

Donna Martonfi

Mar. 1/15

Copyright: Donna Martonfi
110 East River Road
Paris, Ontario N3L 3E1

Website: www.donnamartonfi.com
E-mail: ClimbingHigherDM@aol.com

All rights reserved. This publication may not be reproduced, stored in a retrieval system, or transmitted in whole or in part, in any form or by any means, electronic, mechanical, photocopying, recording or otherwise, without the prior written permission of the Author.

Joshua 1:9

Have not I commanded thee?

Be strong and of good courage;

be not afraid, neither be thou dismayed:

for the Lord thy God is with thee

whithersoever thou goest.

I dedicate this book to...

four very special and most amazing men;

... my darling husband, Darko

who has faithfully been at my side since I was 15 and he was 19.
We have been through many fires, floods and storms and it has just made us stronger
and our love deeper.

... to my incredibly wonderful three sons;

Dan, Mike and Steve

who make my life richer, fuller and so incredibly meaningful.
It is such a privilege and honor to be your mom.

ACKNOWLEDGMENTS

Every month I had a deadline to meet when writing these article. Many were written at very odd hours dependent upon when my creative juices would begin to flow. So, my profoundest 'thank you' goes to Penny Oliver DelZotto who was my living, breathing, walking, talking, call-any-time-of-the-day-or-night Thesaurus who helped me tweak so many of these articles by suggesting better adjectives, verbs and pronouns. She certainly makes me sound as if I have an incredibly proficient command of the English language.

I would also like to thank my very techno-savey hero, Ken Haines, who spent many hours converting these articles into PDF files, making them ready for publishing.

A special 'Thank You' goes to my dear friend, Laurie Lessard, who coordinated the back cover.

Last, but not least, is my new friend, Irma-Joy Tinus, whom I feel as if I have known my entire life. We are so much alike in the spirit that knew, that I knew that she was the artist that the Lord brought into my life to do the cover of this book.

INDEX

Chapter 1:	A Voice So Bad, Even God Couldn't Stand It
Chapter 2:	Thou Shalt Not Be Tardy or ..... 100,000 Angels
Chapter 3:	The Worst Day of My Life
Chapter 4:	Blue Bathroom Scales Come at Great Expense...The Love of God
Chapter 5:	Go Call Pastor Hardy!
Chapter 6:	Our Streets Are Not Paved With Gold …Or Are They????
Chapter 7:	How Does God Spend His Time?
Chapter 8:	Thou Need Not Be Miserable
Chapter 9:	And Then God Said…
Chapter 10:	It Should Be On The Six O'clock News
Chapter 11:	The Invisible God Becomes Visible
Chapter 12:	If You're Gonna Have a Fight At Least Have It In Public
Chapter 13:	His Resurrection Power Brings Eternal Life
Chapter 14:	Just a Guy In a Box
Chapter 15:	What's Behind the Mask?
Chapter 16:	Are You Looking For The Perfect Gift?

Chapter 17:	What Does It Take To Get YOUR Attention?
Chapter 18:	Dial 911 ..... Two Little Sparrows Have Fallen
Chapter 19:	What's God Doing at a Garage Sale? ... Shining Through
Chapter 20:	If You've Heard This Message, ...You Will See My Point
Chapter 21:	Why Should I Let Physics Mess Up My Faith
Chapter 22:	I Can Hear the Sound of the Abundance of Rain
Chapter 23:	No Apology On This Menu, Just Some Humble Pie
Chapter 24:	When God Sees His Face --- You're Done
Chapter 25:	A Proven Remedy and a Sure Cure – Son-Shine
Chapter 26:	It's Never a Mistake When You Listen to God's Prompt
Chapter 27:	Why Am I Sitting Here When I Could Be Getting Rich?
Chapter 28:	God is Talking --- Is Your Heart Listening?
Chapter 29:	A New Twist On The Twenty-third Psalm
Chapter 30:	Just a Little Spark Can Set Your Life Ablaze
Chapter 31:	An Ounce of Humor Accomplishes More Than a Pound of Wrath

Chapter 32:	God Will Send Fire From Heaven ... Or Whatever Else You Decree
Chapter 33:	Abandon Your Cave ... Move to Higher Ground
Chapter 34:	Does An Angel Have To Kick You?
Chapter 35:	Have I Got a Deal For You!
Chapter 36:	A Crown of Glory That Fadeth Not Away
Chapter 37:	There Is Only One Solution For These Chaotic Times
Chapter 38:	God Has Stopped Talking To Me ... Now He's Actually Shouting!
Chapter 39:	Don't Cry Over Spilled Milk ... God Has Something Better
Chapter 40:	Heavenly Peace
Chapter 41:	God Cleaned Up My Attitude With a Bar of Soap
Chapter 42:	A Tribute to Christians, Past and Present
Chapter 43:	God's Guarantee Has a Never-Ending Warranty
Chapter 44:	God Certainly Has My Undivided Attention!
Chapter 45:	Jesus Loved to Tell Stories
Chapter 46:	A Miracle is About to Happen
Chapter 47:	Santa's Gift to Jesus

Chapter 48:	She Has the Problem ...But God Fixes Me
Chapter 49:	However Painful, Upon Request, Relinquish To It's Rightful Owner
Chapter 50:	So, How Was YOUR Week?
Chapter 51:	Don't Just Pretend To Be My Friend
Chapter 52:	One God, One Mind, One Message
Chapter 53:	"....Ye have not, because ye ask not"
Chapter 54:	Why Don't I Do This More Often?
Chapter 55:	It's really 'no big deal' for God
Chapter 56:	A Truckload of Grief Destroys My Whole Week
Chapter 57:	'Seek Ye First the Kingdom of God...'
Chapter 58:	Let Me Give You God's Cell Phone Number
Chapter 59:	Sing in the Midst of Disaster
Chapter 60:	Usually, Things Are Never What They Appear To Be
Chapter 61:	God's Very Special Gift to You and Me
Chapter 62:	A Tribute to My Dad
Chapter 63:	Jesus Obtained Reconciliation Between God and His Creation

~ 1 ~

A Voice So Bad, Even God Couldn't Stand It

For eighteen years I have prayed to be able to sing on key. For those of you who can sing, this might not seem like an important request, but you see, I love to sing. I have yet to find anyone who loves to hear me. In church, I have had people turn around from two rows away, with pained looks on their faces, querying who was making the awful racket. I have had kids, with their noses all scrunched up, turn around and just stare at me till I stopped.

It's worse than that. This one time my husband and I went on a long drive with our friends, Fred and Carm. We were having such a glorious time, that on the way home I started to sing, "Praise God, Praise God, Praise God, Praise God." Well that night Fred ended up in the hospital in intensive care. The doctor said it was digestive problems but we all suspect it was my singing.

Another time, my pastor's little girl, whom I adopted as my grandchild-by-love, was about two and a half years old when I took her for a walk down by the intracoastal waterway. Naomi and I were walking hand in hand when my heart started to swell with appreciation for the beauty of the palm trees around us and the magnificence of the day. I was grateful to be in Florida and blessed to be loved by this darling child. Like a geyser, that cannot be held back, I threw back my head and gushed, "Praise God, Praise God, Praise God, Praise God." Naomi dropped my hand. She put both her hands in the air like she was pushing back an invisible wall and said, "Donna I love you, but just don't sing. O. K.? Just don't sing!"

When a two and a half year old begs you to stop singing, that's bad. More than bad, actually. Only divine intervention could rectify my dilemma and grant my heart's desire. And wouldn't you know, God did just that.

One Sunday night in church, I was standing next to Judy who was a gifted and strong vocalist and whose voice I knew would overshadow mine, so instead of just mouthing the words to my favorite song, I let loose and sang for real. I immediately noticed that something was very different. My voice had changed. I was not making a horrid noise. It sounded like I was singing on key. I leaned over and asked Judy, "Can you hear me singing?" "Yes", she replied. "Am I singing on key?" "Yes, you are" was her astonishing reply.

I could not wait for the service to end so that I could report to Carolyn that God had just answered my prayer. She used to say, in that Southern drawl, "Honey, you just keep right on asking God, and one day He'll do it!" Of course, she immediately wanted to hear me. Not wanting to make a fool of myself, in case I was mistaken and possibly still sounded like a barnyard animal, I decided I would validate this miracle outside in the driveway. "Praise God, Praise God, Praise God, Praise God".

Carolyn gazed at me like a raccoon stares at headlights and then exclaimed, "Girl, you've got it!" She actually stopped people as they were coming out of the church, pulled them by their sleeve and declared, "You've just gotta hear this!" Those that had previously heard me, and knew the impossibility of any musical sound emanating from my lips, were astounded. Oh the Glory of being able to sing at the top of my lungs and know it is actually pleasurable to the listener.

As you can well imagine, I have almost become obnoxious. I sing everywhere, to everyone. I have no inhibitions. God has given me a most wondrous and marvellous gift and I am going to make certain that anyone within earshot knows about it. I am also a walking, talking, singing billboard, advertising the fact that God answers prayer, as long as we don't give up and stop asking.

~ 2 ~

Thou Shalt Not Be Tardy or ..... 100,000 Angels

I was convinced that God had omitted a commandment. "Thou Shalt Not Be Tardy' should have been number 11. I spent many precious hours watching plants grow, while counting how many hair fell out of my head. I could not understand why people did not allow for the fortuitous or the unforeseen. Most people could resolve a great many of their problems by simply prioritizing, leaving room for the unexpected and honoring their commitments. I would pace and fume and shed, hour upon hour, while waiting for these tardy people to arrive. I developed an attitude, even though they say Godly patience is shown by how you act while you're waiting. I have driven over sidewalks, around mail boxes and in between lamp posts when it looked like I could be the cause of someone pacing a floor for even ten minutes, much less an hour or more. Especially since I thought it might hamper my Christian witness. Christians might get away with an attitude, but no way should they be late.

At the time, I had two overlapping careers. This particular day I had a seven o'clock real estate appointment in Mississauga which was exactly sixty minutes away. Therefore, according to my 'thou-shalt-leave-room-for-the-unexpected' calculations, I planned to leave downtown Toronto, where I was counseling, by no later than 5:20 p.m. Since I had overemphasized to these people that I was a 'Christian', the extra 40 minutes were a mandatory precaution. Jesus was never late. I follow Jesus, therefore I cannot be late.

Life they say is full of the unexpected. About midday, I was asked to try and console a lady who was weeping in the lobby and squeeze her between my appointments. Her problem was paramount and she needed to talk to someone. No Problem! My dilemma occurred though around 4:00 p.m. when another distressed woman came in. The lady was in a state of panic. They came to get me. I panicked. What to do? I was running late. My other appointments started to double up. No Problem ! Jesus never panicked. I'll talk faster. I'll pray faster. I'll walk faster. As long as I get to my car by 6:00 p.m. my Christian witness would stay intact.

Did I say, no problem? There was a major problem. Exiting onto the highway I found one mess of a traffic jam. Bumper to bumper. The cars might as well have been parked. Nobody was going anywhere. I started to feel hair follicles releasing their grip. I decided I had lost too many today, it was time to take decisive action, "Lord God, even if it takes 100,000 angels, please clear this mess!" I was serious. I knew God had more than enough angels waiting in the wings for just such an emergency. This was an emergency. I was a Christian and Christians can not be late. Plus I reasoned, I gave the Lord the extra mile today: two actually, so, I didn't think I was unreasonable in asking for help so I could uphold my integrity.

Just then, out of corner of my eye, I spotted a sight that made me shout and holler, "THANK YOU GOD ! HALLELUIA!" I couldn't believe my eyes. God's s-o-o-o smart! There in my rear view mirror appeared 'one' angel. Not 100,000 angels, just one. But, ... one with authority and power and a way to get me out of this mess. Siren blaring, lights flashing, he was coming up behind me at quite a clip. I jutted into the next lane, out of the cruiser's way and then immediately shot right back in behind him and glued myself to his bumper yelling "Glory Hallelujah!" as cars parted and moved out of his way and we advanced through stand still traffic, all the way to Mississauga. It wasn't a real angel, but it was a genuine miracle. Ahead of me, the officer kept glaring into his rear view mirror wondering what in the world this woman was doing almost attached to his bumper.

I arrived at my destination about 7:20 p.m. only to find that no-one was home. By 8:30 I was almost bald. What was unforeseen here, was that God was going to teach me a valuable lesson.

My clients finally arrived, apologizing because they "-- got stuck in this terrible traffic pile up on the freeway ......" Right there and then, the Lord broke me of not only my compulsion to hurry to make up for lost time, but to not become frantic, ever again. I did not have to hurry. Jesus never hurried. He never had to, because GOD was in CONTROL. He was, is, and always will be.

Scripture says, *"Come unto me, all ye that labour and are heavy laden, and I will give you rest. Take my yoke upon you, and learn of me.....* -- (and all your hair shall still be attached to your head).

~ 3 ~
The Worst Day of My Life

I give the illusion of being a strong, confident, seemingly invincible individual, but it is only because God gave me a strong confident, seemingly invincible pillar of a husband to lean on. Therefore it looks like I can do exploits. Since he was scheduled for surgery in the morning, I was ready to keel right over and just about fall to the ground. I was already leaning 40 degrees.

We had just dozed off when the phone rang. At 1:15 a.m., you know it's not someone bearing good news. We were relieved to find it was an obscene caller rather than the perceived tragedy. I knew if I started telling him about God, he'd not likely call back. I managed to doze off once more. The next intrusive, earth moving sound made us scurry to our feet and set us both in motion, running through the house. The fierce February blizzard, snapped the 70 foot pine tree, directly in front of our house, like a matchstick, crashing it onto our roof. We assessed that most of the damage was over the garage and our belongings and furnishings would not have to be rearranged in the middle of the night. Sleep would now be impossible so we sat drinking coffee, waiting for morning, too tired and too stunned to converse. Neither of us thought to pray. Pity.

After clearing, what must have been three feet of snow off the car, it would not start. I couldn't even pretend at being strong or confident and I was certainly far from seemingly invincible.

At 6:00 a.m. my husband got in his truck and drove himself to the hospital to face his surgical procedure alone. I couldn't drive the truck so, I was left to dial AAA and unravel.

Even though I was placed as top priority on their list, nobody showed up until 1:00 p.m.. They insisted they couldn't find me -- no house, no driveway and no stalled car at the location I gave. I assured them, in the midst of all that snow, was one stressed out, frantic woman, leaning 65 degrees.

My new dilemma was how to find the hospital, in a strange city, with no sense of direction, in the middle of a blizzard with no windshield wiper. Did I neglect to mention that the one on the drivers side blew right off the car? The word hysterical is not a very graphic depiction of the state I was in by the time I arrived at the hospital. Finally I thought to pray.

My husband urged me to leave immediately and go to a repair shop to replace the wiper. This I managed. There were so many people in the service bay, it looked like a close out sale. I was instructed to take a number and to wait because it was going to take a couple of hours. There was no alternative. There was no plan B.

A friend came to mind that lived just minutes away. I called prattling about my misfortune. "Please come and get me, I just can't sit here....I haven't had any sleep..... we had a crank phone call.....a tree hit our house.... my car wouldn't start....my wiper flew off on the highway....it's going to take two hours to fix...." "I rambled all my sentences together. "I need a coffee....."

Without a word of solace, she blurted some lame excuse. If I was finally going to lose it, I would not do it on a pay phone in front of all these strangers. I ran to the bathroom and cried out to God. "HELP ME!"

What I heard back was as clear as if He spoke out loud. "Praise Me!" "Praise You? For what? Don't you understand, this is the worst day of my life!" I persisted hoping for empathy, if not sympathy.

"Praise Me" He continued. "You have no idea how many angels it took to keep and guard you this day. I have kept you safe. The tree did not crush and kill you asleep in your bed. You did not drive into a tree when your wiper flew off. You found the hospital. You know not how many angels were kept busy bearing you up in their arms so you wouldn't dash your foot against a stone."

I stood, hands raised and worshipped God right there in the bathroom. How remarkably extraordinary my day became there in His presence and the revelation of His omnipotence.

~ 4 ~

Blue Bathroom Scales Come at Great Expense...The Love of God

For years and years I was given gifts and presents that looked more like they came from foe rather than friend. I received yellow towels with black stripes and pink towels with green polka dots, even though my bathroom was painted blue. It made you have to hold onto the walls. I wondered if maybe somewhere deep down inside this person really disliked me immensely.

I had a real passion to be color coordinated. I finally attained a financial position in life where I could afford to stick every eyesore gift that I ever got in the back of a closet somewhere and get myself things that matched. I re-did my whole house. The carpets matched the walls and the walls matched the drapes and the drapes matched the bird cage. The bathroom especially became a piece of work with some of my nicest things on exhibit, except for this old, old rusty green bathroom scale sitting in the corner, ruining everything.

Many times a day my eyes would fall on this eye sore that was spoiling this grand display of my talent. I just wouldn't throw it out for fear I would gain a pound.

One day, I found my pastor standing sheepishly at my front door with a gift under his arm.

"Donna" he says, "I wanted to buy you something to thank you for all the help you've been. When I came home with this bathroom scale, Kathy insisted I return it, but wait until you hear what happened. Incidentally, Donna, I am not insinuating that you look like you have need of one."

(I by the way, at that time, was nice and lean and trim, I'll have you know.)

"I was compelled to buy this bathroom scale and as I was standing at the checkout counter, I heard God's voice, as clear as if He spoke out loud say, 'Not BROWN, get BLUE' so I went and exchanged the one I was holding for this blue one."

My mouth hung open as tears filled my eyes and Holy Ghost bumps ran up and down my arms. Such love, I can- not comprehend. I expect and know and truly believe that God will and does answer prayer when I or anybody else has a serious matter that requires the divine hand of God to supervene, as when my eldest son was diagnosed with cancer. We had no less than one thousand people praying across this nation and the Lord spared him from needing chemotherapy or radiation treatments and made him good as new. I thank God for His love and mercy and grace at those times. But when the God who hung the stars in place, who rules the universe, reaches down into my finite, minuscule life and shows me that He cares about the color of my bathroom scale just because it is important to me, it leaves me breathless.

Scripture says, *'Delight thyself in the Lord, and He shall give you the desires of your heart'*.

He also says in His word that He knows the very number of the hairs on our head. This is not to prove His omniscience but rather to show His creation, you and me, how personal a God He is. He wants to be the God of not only our life, but every aspect of our life. He wants to have intimate fellowship with us. He desires to bless us. He knocks at the door of our hearts and yearns to be let in. The choice whether we open that door or not, is ours.

'Delight in Him' means to spend time in His presence and hunger to know Him more. Search His heart and the things that are important to Him and find what path He has set for you to walk.

Blue bathroom scales come at a great price. Jesus paid that price with His life to enable us to be able to seek and find the heart of God and live encompassed by His endless love.

~ 5 ~

Go Call Pastor Hardy!

My friend, Bette, had given me a series of tapes on the person of the Holy Spirit and how our relationship with Him needs to be enhanced. The narrator pointed out the fact that the Holy Spirit is no more a dove or a fire than Jesus is a lamb or a door. He is not some mist or vapor. The Holy Spirit has two hands and two feet and a countenance. He not only indwells the believer, He is the paraclete sent to walk beside us and hold us by our hand. We know these truths but it takes a fresh revelation to illuminate them so that they become an integral part of our being.

I determined to have a closer intimacy with the Holy Spirit. I would sing Him songs of adoration and consult with Him about each and every situation that would arise during the day and really try to have Him orchestrate my every step. I was excited to have this renewed revelation. I wanted to go to a higher level and reach a new plateau in the knowledge of God and my relationship with Him and develop that supernatural, Spirit-lead, ever-conscious-of-the-presence-of-God stance.

I was looking forward to what the day would bring when the Lord simply stated, "Go call Pastor Hardy".

Pastor and Sister Hardy were the two most precious people that God ever put on this good earth some eighty- plus years ago. They were full of joy and love. They walked in meekness, kindness and humility, crowned with a wonderful sense of humor. On top of all that, they were genuine. They made a dramatic impact on anyone that was blessed to have ever crossed their path. They were like our Grandma and Grandpa in the Lord. We loved them dearly.

"I'll just have to call them on Sunday", I thought. Much more feasible because on Sunday my long distance rate to Canada is only five cents a minute.

"Go call Pastor Hardy," the Lord interjected. Well, it just doesn't make sense to call in the middle of the week, so I decided to write them a letter. I acknowledged our love and expressed how greatly they were missed and sealed the envelope.

The Lord again repeated, "Go call Pastor Hardy." Just then a thought came to mind. ´ I should include some of my Psalm 40 bookmarks so they could distribute them to some of the folks in their congregation who knew me. I then resealed the envelope.

I still didn't have peace though, so I came up with another idea. "I'll bless them with an encouraging word of scripture and I also seared out a lovely little poem I knew they would like and resealed the envelope a third time.

"GO CALL PASTOR HARDY."

"Ahhhhh, yes Lord. Right now I'm going to go call Pastor Hardy", I sheepishly replied, now realizing that the Lord WANTED ME TO CALL Pastor Hardy.

I was puzzled that I needed to call today and at the same time agonized that God had to speak to me four times before I complied. I must exasperate God. In the future, I determined to obey at the first request. I mean, I was preaching sermons on obeying the voice of God and the Lord practically had to shout before I responded. If I was going to be resolved to be led of the Spirit, I would need to change this I'm-going-to-do-it-my-way behavior and not be so incredulous no matter how illogical the request seemed. God must have His reasons. I picked up the phone, eager now to find out what they were. "Hello Pastor Hardy, this is Donna." I chirped into the receiver.

"Oh Donna, my dear. How wonderful that you would call. You remembered my birthday. How very sweet. That means so much to me."

~ 6 ~

Our Streets Are Not Paved With Gold

...Or Are They????

The war in Yugoslavia was in full swing the year I quit real estate. My very last clients were Serbian refugees who had saved up enough downpayment to purchase a home. Though I was born in Croatia, I was raised in Canada from the time I was five. I always thanked God and was proud that I was raised in a nation that promoted tolerance and acceptance instead of political bias.

Shortly after this couple settled into their 'dream come true', they became proud parents and repeatedly phoned and invited me to come see God's newest gift to them. This was totally unfeasible. Not because we were from opposing factions, but because at that time I could not afford the gas to drive the 35 miles to their home, much less buy a baby gift. Unfeasible, you say after having a successful career for 24 years? No. Just months before, there was a major crime committed by three unscrupulous, dishonest businessmen. Criminals to be more exact. Their target just happened to be me and my family. Their scam caused us to lose our home, our stocks, our bonds; everything we owned. We were embezzled and when the dust settled, we were left with exactly 39 cents to our name. They went to jail, but we never got our money back.

Friends told us to think positive. "Oh, I'm positive I'm broke", I replied, "and also positive I can't afford to go anywhere or do anything." I was not about to try to explain that to refugees, from a communist country, that believed that money grows on trees in North America and that our streets are paved with gold. So I tried to become unobtrusive while hoping they wouldn´t think I was prejudiced or that I harbored animosity toward them. Feasible? It should have been. But no, they probably wanted to show their absence of hostility and resolved to surpass mine.

"Donna, we figure our daughter will be in college before we get to show her off, so we decided to take a ride to the country and come and see you."

At that moment I became brain dead. I might as well have had a lobotomy. I could not think of one rebuttal. As I hung up the phone I desperately pleaded, "JESUS, YOU HAVE TO DO SOMETHING!" I had no coffee. I had no milk. I had no money. My credit cards were maxed. I had nothing to set on a plate to offer as a sign of friendship and hospitality. I stood stunned, motionless, staring out the window

My hand was still on the receiver when I saw a car drive up, two men climb out, pick up these two motors that were laying on the ground beside our garage, leftovers from a previous garage sale, and place them in their trunk. Then one man reached into his wallet and passed my husband what looked like a lot of bills. They were strangers and they came out of nowhere and they were buying my husband´s junk. I bolted out the door the moment they left, my feet barely touching the ground, calling, "How much? How much did you just get?"

"Eighty dollars!"

"Praise God! God sent angels. They were angels!" I yelled, grabbing the money from his hand and flying toward the car to go buy groceries.

"No Donna, angels would have paid me FULL price. These guys haggled me down to half price."

By the time my honored guests arrived, I had a feast prepared, including chicken soup with dumplings and a choice of desserts.

That was just the beginning of the Lord restoring what the devil had taken through those embezzlers. Again and again the Lord provided and continues to provide exactly what we need, when we need it.

For those that trust in Him, His word says that *'He shall supply all of our needs according to His riches in Glory by Christ Jesus.'* That includes spiritual, emotional, physical, and financial *'............ your heavenly Father knoweth that ye have need of all these things. Behold the birds of the air: for they sow not, neither do they reap, nor gather into barns; yet your heavenly Father feedeth them. Are you not much better (valuable to Him) than they?'*

~ 7 ~
How Does God Spend His Time?

We've all had these various erroneous ideas of what God does. Everything from images of him sitting on a cloud counting angels to Him casting lightning bolts across the sky when irked and provoked. Angels, I assure you, do not get misplaced, therefore an inventory does not have to be taken at the turn of each new century. Now for the dynamics, components and understanding of thunder and lightning, you'll have to consult your nearest encyclopedia because time and space and my limited knowledge do not permit for an in-depth expose here.

To obtain knowledge and understanding and a concise portrayal of God's attributes, though, we need to turn to another book. Psalm 121 tells us that He never slumbers nor sleeps, while Psalm 3 says, *"But thou O Lord are a shield for me, my glory and the lifter up of mine head. I laid down and slept, I awaked, for the Lord sustained me."* How reassuring that I need not toss and turn all night. I don't need to lose sleep by fretting and worrying since He's going to be up anyway and He is watching over me, sustaining me. It is something that does not come automatically. It took me years to learn to lay my problems at His feet and go to bed with the assurance that He is in control and that He is working out all things for my good and His glory and that nothing is outside of His divine providence.

He states that two sparrows are sold for just a few pennies and not one of them falls on the ground without Him knowing, so to not fear because we are of more value than many sparrows. I can be confident that He will give me the wisdom, the guidance, the direction, plus the solution, for each and every obstacle that occurs in my life because it also says that He will perfect all which concerns me. Great liberty and peace of mind come with that awareness of His omnipotence and omniscience.

Psalm 34 gives us greater insight into how He spends His time. It says that *"the eyes of the Lord are upon the righteous, and His ears are open unto their cry"* and that *"the steps of a good man are ordered by the Lord: and He delighteth in his way."* Who are these righteous? I´m glad you asked. They are those that are in right standing with Him. How do we obtain right standing? By *"confessing with our mouth that Jesus Christ is our Lord and by believing in our heart that God hath raised Him from the dead, we shall be saved. For with the heart man believeth unto righteousness, and with the mouth confession is made unto salvation."* (Romans 10: 9 & 10). He made it so incredibly easy.

God is not only busy guiding and caring for His people, he is busy supplying our needs. I have written on this subject before, but I will quote it again: *"My God shall supply all of your needs according to His riches in glory by Christ Jesus."* That includes financial, physical, spiritual and emotional.

He is busy giving peace. *"Thou wilt keep him in perfect peace, whose mind is stayed on thee; because he trusteth in Thee."* Those who trust in Him, whose thoughts are turned to the Lord, will live with incredible peace. Peace of mind, peace of heart and peace in the midst of any storm even when it looks like your ship is about to sink.

Finally, most everyone knows Psalm 23, where He states that He walks with us, especially when we walk through the valley of the shadow of death. We do not need to fear any evil because

His rod and His staff comforts us. When faced with illness, surgery or the death of a loved one, His solace soothes our pain. He adds in Isaiah 49 that *"He comforts His people, and will have compassion upon them in their sorrow."* Another Isaiah scripture says, *"Fear thou not: for I am with thee; be not dismayed; for I am thy God; I will strengthen thee, yea, I will help thee: yea, I will uphold thee with the right hand of my righteousness."*

God spends ALL of His time caring for us and walking with us through ALL the circumstances of life. It's a very big job. I'm glad He didn't think I was a waste of time.

~ 8 ~

Thou Need Not Be Miserable

Have you got problems? Troubles? Difficulties? Is there a thick, dark cloud hovering overhead, raining giant drops of despair and sadness? You raise your umbrella but still get drenched because the acidity has eaten right through the silk and you're standing there holding only the aluminium skeleton. Are you just plain miserable? Is your smile pasted on your face, intended to mask the heavy ache that's squeezing your heart? Are you tormented by circumstances that are robbing you of sleep?

My own advise would be to not count sheep, but to talk to the Shepherd. The Apostle Paul, in the book of Philippians, has an even better solution. Paul instructs us to *"Rejoice"*. He actually says it twice, *"Again I say, rejoice."* Yes, rejoice. Be glad. Praise God.

You're probably thinking, 'You must be kidding!"' No, I'm not. Don't stone me. This simple, precious truth; this jewel from scripture, is the ultimate remedy that will end your misery. Paul continues, "Don't worry about anything, instead, pray about everything; tell God your needs and thank Him for His answer. If you do this, you will experience God's peace, which is far more wonderful than the human mind can understand. His peace that will keep your thoughts and your hearts quiet and at rest."

We all have problems, troubles and difficulties at one time or another but our inner attitude does not have to reflect our outward circumstance. When Paul was exhorting the Philippians to rejoice, he did not have reason to rejoice. Not only was he in a Roman jail at the time, the emperor, Nero, was throwing

Christians to the lions. He was impaling them on stakes and lighting them on fire and using them as human torches to light his banquets. The possibility existed that Paul could be executed, yet he urged, 'rejoice'. He knew that no matter what his immediate happenstance, Christ was in his heart and he was heaven-bound. He knew the secret ingredient. His destiny was set, for all eternity.

Paul knew from experience. About ten years earlier, he and Silas were in jail, and they were singing praises to God, in spite of their circumstances, and suddenly there was a great earthquake. The prison was shaken to its foundation and the doors flew open and the chains of every prisoner fell off. And Paul and Silas preached the gospel to the jailer and he and his whole household became believers in Christ.

You don't need to live in a prison of despair. Start singing and worshipping God and watch the chains that have you shackled fall off. Your heart and soul and spirit will be set free. Allow His light to illuminate the darkness. The clouds will lift and the sky will become blue again. The sun will begin to shine. You can throw out that silly umbrella. Joy will begin to well up within your spirit and you will want to sing........ SING? Yes. I can attest from experience. It took me years to learn to stop worrying and fretting, which resolves absolutely nothing anyway, and to start singing praises to God instead. Scripture says, *"God inhabits the praises of His people"* -- not the complaints.

I also realized that God is in control and that He brings a resolution to each and every problem. He is working on your behalf. He has promised to work ALL things out for your good and for His glory. It might not happen instantly but it will happen and in the interim your life will be rich and meaningful and you will instead be like a beacon, shining brightly so that the world can see the light of Christ in you.

There is a story about Solomon when he was just a little boy playing in a courtyard and saw the goldsmith pacing back and forth crying, "Woe is me, woe is me. The emperor will have my head". Little Solomon wanted to know why the man was so distressed. The goldsmith told him that the emperor had given him an impossible task to fulfill. He wanted the goldsmith to make him a ring, which when the emperor was happy and looked at it, would make him sad, and if he looked at it when he was sad, it would make him happy. "That's easy!" said little Solomon, "write on it, 'THIS TOO SHALL PASS'."

Be encouraged, "this too shall pass" and until then, rejoice. Your circumstance is about to change!

~ 9 ~

And Then God Said...

I was scheduled to speak in a church in Hamilton, Ontario this past Sunday. As usual, I spent days in preparation; praying, fasting and seeking God's will for the service. "What is it Lord, that you want to say to these people, at this time?" I queried. The pastor had already given a strong indication of what she felt would meet the need of her congregation. I fully agreed and had my message prepared and polished and rehearsed. I was confident that I had a powerful message and that the Holy Spirit would meet every need of each person there.

I got up on Sunday and headed for the shower. Time was of the essence and I didn't have a moment to spare. Why would I need any extra time? What could possibly happen on the way to the shower? Lots, if the shower is 250 feet from where you live. I stay in a trailer on a 300 acre farm which is also used as a retreat for pastors that need to get away and spend time alone with God. Not more than half a dozen people, at most, stay there at any one time. The water pressure in my trailer is so low that I use the shower facilities in the main building instead. I figured I would quickly slip over and not run into anyone at that time of day.

As I entered the building, I heard voices in the main dining room. I lowered my gaze towards the floor, as if that would somehow make me invisible and tried to scurry past. My hair was not combed. Yesterday's makeup was smeared on my face and my teeth were not brushed. Something the cat dragged in would have looked more presentable. "Donna, I watch you on television every Tuesday. How nice to meet you.!" Good grief! I flashed a Cheshire cat grin and then tried to hide behind the big bath towel I was carrying. Caught at my very worst, I muttered some nicety and tried to slip away only to have the owners of the farm grab my arm and usher me into the presence of their guests. One of the gentlemen started to relay that his wife had left him and taken their little boy. The loss of his son was more than he could bear. He was feeling very lonely. God, though, met him in a dramatic way and gave him a powerful song. A song that spoke of God's loss: 'and what God didn't do...... He didn't save His only son, He left him there for you'. Everyone insisted I sit down and have him sing it for me.

As he sang and played the guitar I started becoming anxious, not to mention increasingly embarrassed at my appearance. I was really pressed for time, and even though it was a very moving piece, I was getting behind schedule. I needed to get ready for church. I encouraged them all to come and hear me preach and then left.

I made it to church in plenty of time and as I arrived, a gentleman named Greg came up and introduced himself to me and handed me a poem. He just knew the Lord wanted me to have it. As I read the words, I became overcome with emotion. They were almost identical to the words of the song that was sung to me as I sat in my bathrobe just hours before. Earlier, I had been too preoccupied to hear what the Spirit of God was trying to say to me. I now heard the message loud and clear. God wanted to minister to people that were hurting and suffering the loss of a loved one. Those that were lonely. He wanted to do something extraordinary in that service and I got out of His way and let Him.

Half way through my message, I sensed that the Lord would have me read the poem. John, who wrote the song, did come to the service with his friends and with his guitar. He said he knew in his spirit that I would ask him to play . I did. There was hardly a dry eye in the place. God started to move among the people and began to minister to hurts and to bathe us in His love. Church lasted 4 1/2 hours. It was incredible. It wasn't prepared, polished or rehearsed. Instead, it was a tremendous move of God and church truly became a 'hospital for the brokenhearted'.

To give you a small glimpse of the glory that we experienced and the message that blessed our hearts, I am including the poem in this article. It is the same poem that was posted on the wall at the Oklahoma city bombing site. It is entitled, "And God Said".

I said, "God I hurt."

And God said, "I know."

I said, "God I cry a lot."

And God said, "That is why I gave you tears."

I said, "God I am so depressed."

And God said, "That is why I gave you sunshine."

I said, "God life is so hard."

And God said, "That is why I gave you loved ones."

I said, "God my loved one died."

And God said, "So did mine."

I said, "God it is such a loss."

And God said, "I saw mine nailed to a cross."

I said, "God, but your loved one lives."

And God said, "So does yours."

I said, "God, where are they now?"

God said, "Mine is on my right and yours is in the light."

I said, "God, it hurts."

And God said, "I know."

~ 10 ~

It Should Be On The Six O'clock News

But it's not. That's how I got to be 32 years old and didn't know what was happening right under my nose. Then suddenly, one day, I happened to walk through the doors of a church and discovered the best kept secret in town. God was in the house. I experienced His presence. It felt like I'd stuck my finger in an electrical light socket. Electrical currents were skipping up and down my body and it felt like every hair on my head was sticking straight out in all directions. I felt electrified. It crossed my mind that maybe they wired the pews and carpet. You know, for effect. It's possible. What else could it be?

My son Dan, who was 11 years old at the time, said, "We have to come back here next Sunday" with much emphasis on 'have to'. Astonished I asked, "Did you feel something too?" Then I thought, sure he did, he's sitting on the same pew with his feet on the same carpet. That's when his younger brother Steve shouted, "I feel God in here!" At that moment I saw something incredible. Something I had never seen before in my life. I saw people worshipping God. Oh I had been in and out of churches before. I had seen people having church. I had seen a lot of religious practices and taken part in various rituals but I had never been any place where God was actually present and people were adoring Him. Everyone's eyes were closed and their hands were lifted toward heaven and they were oblivious to me or any sensation I might have been experiencing. They were immersed in God. They were basking in His glory and having fellowship with Him. There was an unspeakable joy. An unexplainable peace. A holy hush.

I didn't think that God came to church. He wasn't in any I had ever attended prior to that day. I have found a very long poem which has become my favorite and I have read it in pulpits across this country. It very aptly apprises that there are cities full of churches, which have great learned preachers who have more than enough refinement and education. They also have the best of talent, wonderful choirs, expensive organs, and produce grand music. They have plans and schemes and programs and many good, honest, eager workers who labor hour by hour and give their time and money unselfishly yet they are missing the very essence of God. Though all these things are excellent and commendable, it concludes that neither worldly wisdom, skill, nor human innovation can bring true repentance nor break the sinner's heart. It is only the Holy Spirit that quickens our soul, exposes our sinful nature, shows us our need for a Savior and reveals Jesus, the Author and Finisher of our faith.

Jesus said in John Chapter 14 that when He goes to be with the Father, *'He would not leave us comfortless, but that He would give us another Comforter, that He may abide with us forever; even the Spirit of truth, whom the world cannot receive, because it seeth him not, neither knoweth Him; for He dwelleth with you and shall be in you'.*

When that same church was sold and before we could move to our newly constructed building, we had to hold services in a highschool auditorium in the interim. I remember walking into the school gymnasium, with its basket-ball nets and bleachers for pews and want to take off my shoes because of the sense that the ground I was standing on was holy ground. A few times I wept because the presence of God was so real and so intense. In a gym, yes, because the Spirit of the living God had preceded me there.

Don't mistake the Holy Spirit for some mist or vapor. He is a person. He is the Third Person of the Trinity. God the Father is on His throne. Jesus is seated at His right hand but it's the Holy Spirit that has been sent 'to' us. He comes where He is invited. He comes where He is welcomed. He comes where hearts are hungry and yearning to have fellowship with Him. Is He at your church?

~ 11 ~
The Invisible God Becomes Visible

During the months that I stay in Canada, I host a live, two hour, call-in television program called Nite-Lite which is produced by and at '100 Huntley Street' which is Canada's largest television ministry. I was first approached to host this program back in the 80's when I was still very young, not in years, but in my Christian walk. I was informed that my only training would be to watch the program for a couple of weeks and get a feel for the type of calls and the variety of subjects and questions that the viewers would present.

The first time I watched, the host was asked, "Isn't the Bible just a glorified history book written by a bunch of men?" Oh, that's my forte, I thought. I could answer that! I had innumerable books and many articles stating that what we have just discovered in the 1900's, has been clearly expounded in the Bible centuries ago. For instance, it clearly states that the blood of animals is different from humans. The blood of all races is the same. The blood of a dead person is lethal. The skin is formed first on the embryo, not the bones. The components which make up our skin and bones are the identical components which are found in earth.

Moses wrote that God created man from the earth. It took science 3,500 years to discover what God gave him divine knowledge of way back then. Many of the purification rituals and instructions pertaining to sanitation prevented the spread of microscopic germs and thwarted infections and disease.

The Word of God is also the most accurate and authoritative historical document ever written. The more advanced we become in this generation, the more proofs we uncover. Excavations at the city of Jericho confirm that it's walls did not fall in but that they were pushed down flat as recorded in the book of Joshua. Then scientists discovered dense vegetation under the ice caps of the north and south poles, meaning the planet was engulfed with moisture such as occurs in a terrarium.

When Noah proclaimed that water was going to fall out of the sky and they were all going to drown, they rolled in the streets laughing because they had never seen rain. Satellite pictures show a large, rectangular object, approximately 450 feet long, perched under the ice and right on top of Mount Ararat, exactly where the bible says Noah's Ark landed. I'm not a rocket scientist, but in my humble estimation, this data alone leaves me with only one possible conclusion.

Another irrefutable fact is that there are thousands of detailed prophecies foretold throughout scripture and that most of them have been fulfilled, at the precise time and at the very place and to the most exact detail. Only God can foretell the future and be 100% accurate. The Apostle Peter stated that 'no prophecy of the scripture came about by the prophet's own interpretation. For the prophecy came not in old time by the will of man; but holy men of God spake as they were moved by the Holy Ghost.' and Timothy expounded ' *all scripture was given to us by inspiration from God*' God said it, I believe it -- that settles it!

I also could have added that there is well documented evidence by Dr. Ivan Panin that is absolutely fascinating and proves the Bible is truly the divinely inspired Word of God due to the discovery of hidden numeric codes beneath the Hebrew text of the Old Testament. To have occurred by chance or by human intervention is deemed impossible. Nor does this same phenomenon happen in any other literature.

There are volumes full of information available for anyone to be able to intelligently ascertain that the Bible was written by a supernatural intelligence. God would not have created us and then neglected to include the instruction manual. I would have probably taken up most of the program trying to prove this to that caller, but the host that night gave the most profound answer, "Just look at the change in the lives of those that read it and believe it" Bingo!

"For the word of God is quick and powerful and sharper than any two-edged sword, it penetrates even to dividing soul and spirit, joints and marrow; it judges the thoughts and attitudes of the heart.' God also says of His word, *'it shall not return unto me void, but it shall accomplish that which I please and it shall prosper in the thing whereto I sent it.'* It has within itself the power for it's own fulfillment.'

A few years ago I was encouraged to quote scriptures out loud that pertained to my immediate circumstances until God's will was manifested in my life. Not only did this revolutionize my life , but approximately ten days after I started this practice, my friend Yvonne, who is a Baptist minister , was praying for me and she suddenly exclaimed, "Oh Donna, God is showing me there is a huge flaming sword over your life!" What I was doing in the physical reflected in the spirit realm, probably from the very instant I started praying the scriptures.

I encourage you to read it for yourself and watch it not only transform your life but it will give you the answer for every physical, psychological or spiritual dilemma that you face, and more importantly, it will give you insight into the very nature and character and heart of God . An invisible God will become visible

~ 12 ~

If You're Gonna Have a Fight At Least Have It In Public

You are probably already asking, "You had a FIGHT ? In PUBLIC?" I did. I relish being different. Unpredictable too. This at least has always kept my friends on their toes. My husband on the other hand has just learned to grin and ignore it.

This was not a 'fight' fight, it was really only a loud argument. Not even your typical ordinary argument, as my friend Fiona and I found out. I met Fiona one day when she happened to stumble into a prayer meeting. God had never been an integral part of her life. She wasn't even certain that He existed, but had come to investigate, nevertheless.

She developed an instant appetite for the things of God. She rattled off questions faster than we could answer them. Reminded me of myself. I liked her instantly. Since this one meeting could not even begin to satisfy her hunger nor the fire that was ignited in her soul, I invited her to a donut shop where I attempted to fill in the blanks all the way from the book of Genesis right through to Revelation. All in one sitting, yet. It is possible. I've tried it many times. (smile) I have a propensity for dragging people off to restaurants, until the wee hours of the morning, trying to teach them everything I know. With Fiona, it all stuck.

She became a carbon copy. I would start a sentence and she could finish it. Mostly, we just both talked at the same time, because it saved time. We were continuously busy telling everyone, everywhere, all the time, about the Lord. We were a great team, with a lot of zeal and much passion.

One day the pupil surpassed teacher and that's when this argument occurred. My book was hot of the press and Fiona had just read an excerpt that she was thought was all wrong. She was convinced that she had given a particular insight to a group of ladies instead of me. For more than an hour we sat in a fast food restaurant battling it out, oblivious to anyone around us. We sat facing each other, holding hands across the table, and as was our bent, we both talked at the same time, each trying to vehemently persuade the other that 'she' was right.

When I told her to close her eyes and recall how the leader of the group had asked me to stop, she realized that it would have had to be me speaking. Tears burst from her eyes as she agreed that she had been wrong and couldn't understand why she remembers making those remarks. We concluded that it was because she was such a good student and had probably used the same references either at work or someplace else. I'm certain you can envision the scene that followed

Our rambling was abruptly halted when a discomfiting voice interjected, "This can not be happening! I did not hear what I think I just heard!"

Startled we turned in the direction of the unexpected intrusion. The comments were coming from a spiffy looking lady who was obviously a business woman because she was packing a briefcase, a pager and a car phone. She seemed visibly astonished.

"The two of you have just re-arranged my day. I'm not going back to work. I'm going home to think about what I just witnessed. I have never heard or seen such love. This is unreal."LOVE ??? We were having a fight!

Fiona, being the great protégé, scoots over to this ladies' table and starts gushing about Jesus and His love. Like an Artesian well she just started splashing all over this woman. I ran to the car to retrieve a copy of my book for this potential reader.

You must have already guessed the rest. That lady never did get to work that day. Fiona and I, trying NOT to talk at the same time, fed her a dose of God's Word, trying to cover everything from Genesis all the way to Revelation.

I emphasize the word trying. But, that lady's life did change that very day. Fiona got her phone number and continued to mentor a brand new believer in the ways of God, just as she had seen me do for her. They became friends, too.

"A new command I give unto you; that you love one another. As I have loved you, so you must love one another. All men will know that you are my disciples if you have love one to another."
John 13: 34 & 35

Ephesians 5:2 *"Be imitators of God, therefore, as dearly loved children and live a life of love, just as Christ loved us and gave Himself up for us ....."* yadda, yadda, yadda.

~ 13 ~

His Resurrection Power Brings Eternal Life

The teacher at school explained that Easter weekend was a special event whereby God demonstrated His love for the whole world. At nine years of age, I could not relate that to the shocking cruelty I encountered at home that Easter Sunday morning. A devastating scene took place. It left a scar on my fragile nine year old spirit and a lasting painful memory that brought sadness far beyond what a child should bear. Easter became associated with that unpleasantness.

By the age of fourteen, and now in high school, I discovered Easter weekend hosted two very important events, the Easter Parade and the fashion show. My after- school job supplied the new spring coat and the latest bonnet. Hats were the high fashion. Sophistication was the craze and every teenage girl sported her Audrey Hepburn hat to church. These hats sat so low over the eyes that the only thing showing between the shoulder blades and the brim of the hat were our lips. The older girls had cigarette holders poised between their pearly whites but at fourteen, two and a half inch spike heels were as far as you dared to go. Smoking would have to wait til at least fifteen. Easter had potential.

By the age of nineteen, this national holiday allowed for additional R & R with friends. Nothing more. Nothing less. Easter was now just convenient.

By the age of twenty-five I had three babies, mortgage payments and loads of dirty laundry. Easter weekend evolved into three days of catching up on much needed rest. Wearing your robe and slippers til noon was now the venue.. Sophistication was dead. Casual was in. Did I say casual? Flower children, love beads and holes- in -your -clothes created a bottom of the barrel fashion scene. The kids and I sat on the floor and painted eggs. Easter, I was determined, would become a positive, wholesome memory.

By the age of twenty-nine, class and prestige prevailed. Goals changed to keeping up with the Jones´ and buying all the bells and whistles, perks and toys. Working Easter weekend brought my husband triple pay. Easter became profitable.

Finally, at 32 years of age, the reality of Easter dawned in my heart. The true purpose of Easter was revealed to me for the first time. I beheld the Lamb of God who died for the sins of the world and He transformed my life. God became real. God became personal. The Lord of Easter Sunday morning had been waiting all these years to arise triumphant in my life and have His resurrection power bring true life and true meaning to mine.

That grade four teacher was right after all, Easter truly demonstrates God´s love for this whole world. God came to earth as a man to reconcile mankind to Himself. The Creator sweat drops of blood knowing the agony that awaited Him at the hands of His creation, yet He laid down His life willingly so that you and I could have eternal life. Soldiers mocked Him and struck Him with their fists. They flogged Him and spit upon His face because He called Himself the Son of

God. Iron spikes were hammered into his hands and feet at a place called Golgotha, yet He endured the pain and the shame. His side was pierced with a sword while a crown of thorns pierced His head, yet He cried, *"Father, forgive them for they know not what they do."* His blood was shed for the remission of our sins as He took our penalty upon Himself and paid our debt on that rugged cross. The GLORY and WONDER of it all was that He did not remain on that cross nor in the grave. He rose from the dead and lives forevermore, seated at the right hand of God the Father, interceding on our behalf. His plea to us is that we believe on Him and make Him the Lord of our life. He wants to not only live in our hearts but to mend our broken lives, to soothe our pain and heal our hurts and to make us whole. He wants to give us a reason for living and a glorious hope for the future. *"I am the resurrection and the life: he that believeth in me, though he were dead, yet shall he live . And whosoever liveth and believeth in me shall never die."*

Right now, this very minute, why don't you ask Jesus Christ to arise in your heart and make Himself real to you? Don't wait another year. He loved you so much that He died to make this Easter weekend a BLESSED, GLORIOUS, and ETERNAL celebration of His endless love.

~ 14 ~

Just a Guy In a Box

Thanksgiving is on Thursday, so I'm certain you presume I would be expounding and extolling all our many blessings and reminding folks just how much we take for granted in this great country. I should be writing about family gatherings and turkey dinners, but I'm not. Nope. I don't believe I could make one creative statement or add one original comment to the many that have been written over the years on these deserving topics. Instead, this Thanksgiving holiday I would like to tell you about an extraordinary man I met this past summer in Atlanta.

His name is Joe Oreskovic and he is a television producer. He has not always been a television producer. Not many years ago, he lived in a cardboard box on the streets of Atlanta. He never intended to end up living in a box, but then, neither did the other 40,000 homeless people in that city. He had a family, a good job, a large home, a double car garage and all the other perks and whistles. One day, something went wrong. Very wrong. Joe became a non- person with a non-identity. Even drugs and alcohol could not deaden the pain and humiliation. Loneliness, despair and hopelessness were his constant companions. For all intent and purposes, he did not even exist. People scurried past his makeshift shelter and nobody seemed to care.

All those months, he didn't know that God cared. Cared very much. Cared enough to send a firefighter to tell him about Jesus. This good Samaritan gave Joe not only a meal, but food for his soul. He gave him 17 scripture verses that became his life-line and his hope. Then a police officer took him to a rehab center and encouraged him to get a job mopping floors at a fast food chain. These two seemingly simple acts of kindness altered his life forever.

Joe got his life back on track and became determined to find a way to repay the firemen and the law enforcement officers of this entire nation. God gave him a vision to build a Memorial Garden in their honor. People laughed out loud, when the guy from the box, spoke of raising two million dollars. Joe heard that Jesus fed the 5,000 with just a few loaves and fishes and realized that Jesus simply used what was available to Him, a little boy's meager lunch. After blessing this meal, He merely distributed it, and everyone had more than enough. So, Joe took what he had, a mop and gargantuan faith and believed God for a miracle.

After meeting the owner of a two acre property and then pre-selling cemetery plots to raise the funds, Joe made God's Word come alive.

The Public Servant's Memorial Garden, in Atlanta, with the 17 scriptures engraved in granite stands as a testimony that little things become monumental when God is in them.

Joe is also solely responsible for orchestrating House Bill 1033 which introduced the 20 year retirement program for the firemen and policemen of Georgia.

Joe then enhanced God's vision by going back to his place of deprivation, via television, and reached out a helping hand. In this past year, his program, the Gravedigger, a nickname that stuck because of the cemetery plots, has been responsible for directly stopping 2 murders and 12 suicides through it's suicide prevention hotline .Remarkably, over 100 people have testified that they came off alcohol and drugs because of the guy that came out of a box.

Joe understands the concept of giving thanks. He learned it from two government servants who saw him as more than an occupational hazard. Giving thanks is not just some warm fuzzy sentiment on a family holiday. It is reaching out, as servants of the living God, to those around us, with what He has placed in our hand and doing unto others..

Part of a song we sing in church fitly says :

Touch through me, Holy Spirit, Touch through me.

Let my hands reach out to others, Touch through me

Love through me Holy Spirit, Love through me

I will be my brother's keeper, Love through me.

Hearts are bleeding deep inside,

Love can dry their weeping eyes,

So love through me Holy Spirit, Love through me.

Happy ThanksGIVING. May you give as you have received -- bushels of blessings.

~ 15 ~

What's Behind the Mask?

I am going to get myself into some hot water here. I really am. I have done it before and undoubtedly will do it again but for some reason I always go where angels fear to tread. I should have written this article last April, on my way OUT of town, instead of a couple of weeks before I am to arrive BACK to Venice but in a minute you will understand why I'm writing this today at this time. You'll not likely be reading much about this subject anywhere else. I am going to give you enough startling facts and information that will hopefully cause you to wake up and smell the coffee!

Increasingly, in this day and age, parents and grandparents are concerned. Very concerned. There is much to be concerned about. Our kids are being targeted and bombarded at every turn by media and material that lowers their morals and standards and values . Why is it then that so many parents, who have taught their kids since they could walk and talk,to not under any circumstances ACCEPT CANDY FROM STRANGERS, then do a 180 degree turn and are coerced into everything and anything that society, Hollywood or whoever puts across to our children as a normal, as an acceptable and as an inevitable event that we dare not question? Why do we then allow, even festively encourage, them to celebrate Satan's holiday?

That is precisely what Halloween is. Ironically, it is one of the two holidays that public schools celebrate because they insist there is no 'religious' significance. There is no Christian significance but it is a pagan religious day, nonetheless, rooted in the worst kind of pagan rituals and worship. It is the Celtic Festival of Samhain, lord of death and evil spirits, originating back 2,000 before Christ and celebrated by Wiccans (witches). Their dark ceremonies led to gruesome deaths. Druid priests would go from house to house asking for fatted calves, black sheep and human beings which were then sacrificed to appease evil spirits. Amid the screaming and torture, while these people and animals where burned to death, observers would dress in costumes and dance and chant and jump through the flames in hope of warding off evil spirits. The lighted faces of Jack O Lanterns were placed on doorsteps as a symbol that damned souls lived in the home while food was offered and left for the spirits as treats so that a curse, or trick, would not be put on the occupant.

It is unimaginable that we are encouraging an observance of this unholy day. Most of the costumes, masks and cardboard cutouts at department stores and supermarkets are not cutsie or funny but depict fiendish creatures that look like they have come from hell itself. Blood-dripping vampires hang from store ceilings and their display racks are crammed with Dracula costumes. Dracula was a real person who lived in the 1400's. He was a demented maniac who massacred 100,000 men, women and children in the most hideous ways. Has he now become a role model? A hero? ' Don't be absurd !', you say? Well, why is his caricature hanging everywhere I look during the month of October? Why are we desensitizing children to the macabre things that shock and horrify? The synonyms for macabre, from Roget's Thesaurus are gruesome, grisly, grim, deathlike, deathly, cadaverous, ghastly, eerie, ghostly, unearthly, weird, dreadful, horrible, and horrific. It is bad enough that fear, mutilation, torture and bizarre murders are glorified through the string of TV programs and videos centering around Halloween, do we need to promote and glorify creatures from beyond the grave? Why take part in this diabolical unholy day? What positive influence will this have in our child's life? Whatever we expose them to will have an effect on their well-being or the destruction of same, whether we admit it or not!

As parents, grandparents and especially as Christians, we need to take what the Word of God says seriously. Ephesians 5:11 states that, *"we are to have no fellowship with the unfruitful works of darkness but rather reprove them",* which not only means expose them, but when I looked up the Hebrew word for 'reprove', the lexical aid used as an example was from Isaiah chapter one; *"Judah,* (the children of Israel) *had been practising religious festivals of their own design in rebellion against God".* The prophet Isaiah called upon them to repent. Repent means a sorrow which results in a change of mind and a change of one's conduct.

Let's not rebel against God but let us repent and LET'S JUST UNMASK HALLOWEEN!

~ 16 ~

Are You Looking For The Perfect Gift?

A couple of our friends were able to come and spend Christmas with us here in Florida one year. Palm trees, sandy beaches, sunshine and good friends. This alone would be reason enough to shout and holler that truly *'my cup runneth over'*. Not according to one of them though who always seemed very concerned about our financial well being.

I assured him I had absolutely everything I could possibly need but he argued that I was living in denial. Peter had watched us revert from a financial success story to losing absolutely everything we owned. We were defrauded out of a great sum of money. The people that cheated us went to jail, but we never got our money back. We now lived on my husband's medical retirement pension and God provided everything else that was needed over and above that. "As a matter of fact," I assured him, "I probably have more shoes right now, in more colors, than I had when we were bringing home the four digit paychecks."

The debate intensified. I could tell that I wasn't scoring points so I reminded them both that my motto was that money could not buy any of the important things in life, just the counterfeit. Money could buy you sex, but not love. Medicine, but not health. Glamour but not beauty. It could buy you a gold watch, but not five minutes of time when you needed it. Therefore, the best things in life were free." My friend obviously did not adhere to this philosophy. Pity.

Oh there was a whole list of things I would like. I could probably go out and spend $25,000 in one afternoon on things that would be nice to have and buy presents for family and friends, but that was not what Christmas was about.

By divine appointment my front doorbell rang and my friend Bette waltzed in all bubbly and cheery and in a very festive mood and handed me this little ornate bag with ribbons hanging from it. Like a little kid I had to open it right away while she ran around the room hugging and kissing everyone. I reached into the bag and when I pulled out the tiny plaque, I started to sob. Now everybody that knows me, knows I NEVER cry. Ever. Somebody has to die before I´ll shed tears. But, I am really crying. Out loud. I mean these gigantic drops of H2O are pouring down my face and everyone´s flabbergasted and wondering ´Why?´.

I could barely believe my eyes. It was incredible. "PETER, PETER, there IS something I have need of, and the Lord just sent it!"

He not only provides what I need, He rings my bell and brings it right to my front door," I sniffed.

Just the week before, I was at the Christian bookstore, reading every plaque and every card and anything that had writing on it, trying to find a certain ´prayer-poem´ that I had stuck on my fridge many years ago. I spent almost two hours looking for it, even though I hate to shop. To me, shopping is synonymous with going to the dentist, but I was determined to find it. I wanted it for my friend Judy who had been going through very difficult times for months. I couldn´t remember all the words, but they were just what she needed to hear and I couldn´t think of anything more special or encouraging for her that Christmas. Eventually I gave up, and left the store very disappointed. On

Christmas Eve, Jesus had it delivered right to my front door. His Christmas present to me. The timing of it's arrival was remarkable. God honored my words. I ran to the phone and called Judy. Through choked words and crackling voice, I read what I knew God needed her to hear.

This same prayer is my Christmas gift to all of you reading this article:

I SAID A PRAYER FOR YOU TODAY

I said a prayer for you today

And know God must have heard

I felt the answer in my heart

Although He spoke no word.

I didn't ask for wealth or fame.

I knew you wouldn't mind.

I asked Him to send treasures

Of a far more lasting kind.

I asked that He'd be near you

At the start of each new day.

To grant you health and blessings

And friends to share your way.

I asked for happiness for you

In all things great and small.

But it was for His loving care

I prayed the most of all.

Two thousand years ago, God presented us all with a most precious gift, Himself. Emmanuel, God with us. The greatest gift you can give to someone this Christmas is to tell them about Him and give them this prayer.

~ 17 ~
What Does It Take To Get YOUR Attention?

So many of you expressed how much you enjoyed my article about Fiona that it has inspired me to tell you about her husband John. I promise you, you will love hearing about him even more. I just wish you could hear him tell this story, with his thick English accent and subtle, dry sense of humor.

I know you would just roll on the floor. You would also not be able to miss the message that God will part the heavens to manifest His love for us. Especially for those of us who don´t yet know Him or know of His glorious love.

First I have to ask you, do I look like a hell, fire and brim-stone preacher? ´Of course not !´, you say, ´ those preachers wear black suits and have handlebar mustaches and wave their bibles high in the air, above their heads, while yelling ´THUS SAITH THE LORD!´

I agree with you. Those are my sentiments exactly. But the truth is, I SOUND like one. I really do. You see, I´m constantly saying, ´it is written´ which is a colloquial for ´thus saith the Lord´ and I often expound, ´You need Jesus to be saved´. You wouldn´t know it to look at me, but I do. I really do.

Sixteen years ago, when I met Fiona and she ´took´ (which is my own translation of her conversion) she begged me to hide my bible when I was around her husband and to not say Hallelujah as much. Her concern was that he would think that she was becoming a fanatic. A word, which by the way means, a fan, or a devoted admirer. N-o-t possible. This was like asking a duck not to swim or a bird not to sing. So, I just continued to wave my King James Version all over Fiona's kitchen.

John, while pretending to hide behind his newspaper in the living room, would be leaning so far towards the kitchen that he would just about topple off his chair trying to hear what it was that we were discussing. Since I knew that Fiona had five churches full of saints praying that John would come to the knowledge of God and ask Him into his heart and life and since I believe to the depth of my being that God answers prayer, I ran in and out of her house proclaiming, "God's going to get you John." Meaning of course, 'You might as well give up John. Just surrender your life to Him now, because, you see John, there are so many people praying for you, asking God to make Himself real to you and reveal Himself to you, that you are just making it difficult on everyone, including God by pretending to be so disinterested and agnostic. God's going to SAVE you, John. You don't stand a chance!' Seemed very reasonable and clear to me!

This scenario continued for nine months. Fiona fervently praying but all the while hiding how often she went to church and how deep her commitment and excitement for the things of God really was. John nonchalantly continued to give the impression he was immersed in the daily news and that he was oblivious to our very presence, yet he was trying feverishly to hear and decipher every word which I was deliberately and loudly projecting his way.

Then unexpectedly, while vacationing at a cottage which had an outside staircase that lead to the second story balcony on which John was standing, he was knocked down the flight of stairs by a bolt of lightening. He wasn't burned. He wasn't knocked unconscious. He was just flat on his back on the ground at the bottom of the stairs. He relates that all he could hear going over and over in his head was 'Donna Martonfi's voice stating, God's GOING TO GET YOU'. Now you all know that is NOT what I meant. John on the other hand, wasn't certain of anything except that he should have been dead, but was not. He deliberated very seriously about God and wondered why his life was spared and about how close he came to dying.

The next day, still very rattled by the incident, he decided to go fishing and mull over events of past, present and future. The lake was quiet, calm and serene. He stopped about the middle and lowered anchor. Out of a clear blue sky, with not a cloud in sight, again a bolt of lightening hit and knocked him right out of the boat, into the water. Again he says he heard Donna Martonfi's voice stating, ' God's going to get you John' Right there in the middle of the lake, he raised his arms toward heaven and shouted, 'God, I'm yours. I'm turning my life over to you."

What are the odds? I'm not even going to pretend to understand the ramifications and complexities of it all. I do know that God loved John tremendously. He loves you and me so much that He came to earth and gave His life selflessly, so that you and I and John can have eternal life. Jesus could have summoned thousands of angels to His aid yet He silently suffered beatings and floggings at the hands of cruel men, while those angels cringed, to pay the penalty of our sin. He willingly laid down His life so that we would not be eternally separated from Him and He reconciled us to Himself through the shedding of His precious blood. He rose again from the dead and sits at the right hand of God the Father, waiting to share His glory with those who call upon His name.

You're probably wondering what's happened to John. Oh he's out there preaching hell, fire and brimstone, advocating 'God's going to GET you!'

Incidentally, did you know that Venice, where I live, is the lightening capital of the world?

~ 18 ~

Dial 911 ..... Two Little Sparrows Have Fallen

Sheila, was on life support, fighting for her life. The prognosis was critical. She was not expected to live. Her car veered out of control on a ramp and ended up on it's roof, totally flattened. The firemen had to use the 'Jaws of Life' to pry her out. She had two small kids. She was very young. Too young to die. For weeks she was at death's door, barely alive and in coma. Relatives arrived from overseas. Arrangements were made for her funeral but against all odds, she survived.

I prepared to go and somehow get her to make things right with God. I decided I should first read up on coma patients because I had heard that they are aware of everything that is going on around them. Too many heartbroken survivors relay how well-meaning visitors talk about them as if they were already dead, refer to them in the third person and end up causing unintentional yet unimaginable hurt and pain.

To everyone's amazement, Sheila came out of the coma. When I arrived at the hospital, she was wrestling with a nurse. Her eyeballs were rotating and she was flailing frantically at the nurse who was trying to keep her from ripping her diaper off. I closed one eye shut tight and yelled out, "SHEILA, PEEK-A-BOO, I SEE YOU!" Jerking her head in my direction, she instinctively mimicked my gesture, cocked her head to one side and closed one eye. Everything went into focus for her for the first time in months. With the world finally not spinning around about her, she calmed down. There was also recognition in that eye. She knew who I was. I realized I just witnessed a major breakthrough. I took hold of both her hands. As long as she kept one eye closed, she remained consoled. If she opened them both, her head would start to spin and she would panic. It didn't take her long to learn to keep one shut.

She had been fed intravenously all this time so the nurse asked if I would try to feed her because I had a calming effect on her. Eat for me she did! Spinach yet! I had more green goop on the bedding than in her stomach but it was a start. I laughed and joked and kept repeating, "Thank God you are alive", knowing it would have an impact on her. Her demeanor changed and a peace and calmness settled upon her. Her eyes spoke volumes as she quizzically peered first out of one, than out the other. Her world stopped spinning. Her stomach was full. She heard people laugh. She soon dozed off.

I determined to come as often as I could. I determined to bring laughter and joy and realized through goosebumps that I could make a difference because her family and friends were traumatized and grief-stricken and mostly cried when they saw her. So, I brought in a cassette tape with a song about a little sparrow falling out of a tree and Jesus picking it up and holding it in the palm of His hand and making it all better. It even had birds chirping in the background. I saw tears in the nurse's eyes every time I played it. The message was very clear. I thought of Matthew 10:31; *"Fear ye not therefore, ye are of more value than many sparrows"*

Before long I was permitted to take Sheila to the cafeteria in a wheelchair. She immediately resisted, obviously aware that her shaved head was not very glamorous. So, I grabbed the bib tied around her neck and pulled it up over her head exclaiming ,

"Perfect! You look like Mother Teresa!" A big grin flashed across her face. When she reached up and felt the headgear she began to glow with esteem. We tied her in the chair and I raced down the hall like a little kid, weaving and whooping it up. Sheila squealed with delight. The nurses and doctors never once motioned for me to stop. They certainly understood what brings health and wellness.

Though Sheila could not speak, she did comprehend quite a bit so I propped my feet up on her bed, leaned back and began reading her a copy of my autobiography. Out of the corner of my eye, I noticed a tall hunk of a man walk in and visit with the lady laying in the other bed . Then, without looking at me, with his four foot shoulders squared, his head pointing straight ahead and his eyes fixed on some distant object, he demanded, "Is that your book?"

"Ummmm, yes" I managed to croak, not knowing what to expect next.

"Are you an author?" he asked without looking in my direction.

"If one book qualifies, I guess I am." I managed to answer.

"Well , I have a chapter for your next book!" he firmly stated.

It threw me for a loop. I wondered why this man would want to contribute some story to my next book and for what strange reason. He continued without waiting for my comment, "You see, my wife ended up in this bed on that very same day Sheila had her accident."

Well, so what, I thought, someone had to occupy that bed.

"That's not all," he said choking back tears, "I was the fireman who was cutting Sheila out of her car at the exact same time my wife was having this stroke."

My heart welled up in my throat. I became choked with emotion when I realized how these two broken little sparrows intertwined and the enormity of this coincidence. Your mind goes numb. You positively KNOW that there is more to this than meets the eye.

"Oh, THERE IS MORE" burst from his lips while tears streamed down his face, "Sheila is our next door neighbor".

~ 19 ~

What's God Doing at a Garage Sale?

... Shining Through

My husband cannot pass up a garage sale. I think his car is programmed to stop at each and every one. As a matter of fact, on our way to the church where I was scheduled to preach one Sunday in South Carolina, he pulls up to one and buys a weedeater and a lawn mower and puts them on top of our luggage. As we drive up to the church, the pastor, who knows we have no grass asks why are we traveling around with a lawn mower and a weedeater?

I'm worried he'll think we have to do landscaping as we go, to pay our way. So I explain how Darko cannot pass up a bargain. Even though we have no grass, the price was right. He gets euphoric because he finds a bargain, not because he finds something he needs. I don't even like to shop. As a matter of fact, I hate shopping. To me, going shopping and going to the dentist are synonymous and a necessary but unavoidable evil. I wish that clothes would just appear in my closet. This is why this particular Saturday afternoon was definitely ordained by God.

Darko came home talking about a thirty-five dollar hope chest that he thinks he should not have passed up. He said that if I wanted it, he'd go back and get it. If I wanted it??? First of all, what do I want with a hope chest at my age? Second, I already have a hope chest. And thirdly, since it was the end of the month, I needed thirty-five dollars more than I needed grass for my lawn mower. Why are we having this discussion I wanted to know?

Later that afternoon, on our way to the restaurant, Darko decided to go back to that same garage sale to see if something else he passed up was still there. I never get out of the car at garage sales. NEVER. I have everything I could possibly need. I do not need one more thing in my life. Nevertheless, that day, I got out of the car. The lady holding the sale recognized Darko and presumed he brought me back to buy the hope chest, so she says, "I can´t do any better than thirty-five dollars."

"Oh no, no no," I blurted, I don´t need a hope chest". At that very moment I sensed God say, "Give her thirty-five dollars for the hope chest." I walked over to my husband and asked him not to haggle. It´s not a bargain to him unless he can get it cheaper. To him it´s a sport. I figure, if it´s worth $100, and they´re asking two dollars, you should give them five. At least!

When she admitted that it was her mother´s but that she was forced to sell it because she needed the money, I knew we should exchange phone numbers in case she was ever in a position to buy it back. I then invited her to see a play in town. She agreed to attend.

True to her word she did come to the presentation but I noticed that she left before it ended so I called her to find out why. The conversation lasted two and a half hours. The whole time we talked about God and how He provided a way for us to have eternal life. She then prayed with me and committed her life to Him.

What she said next was incredible. It left a tremendous impact on me. I was in blue jeans. I was not wearing a robe and sandals. I was not quoting King James nor did I have a copy under my arm. Yet, she said, " I didn't think you were a real person. I thought maybe you were an angel. Your eyes looked right through me. My boyfriend asked me where I was going after you left, and I said I was going to take a shower because I felt dirty".

Folks, the people that are living without God in their lives recognize the GLORY of God that we carry within us. They don't know what it is, but they see it in our eyes. Why don't we see it in each other? Why don't we acknowledge it in each other? If we did, it would have a radical effect on how we act toward each other. How we relate to each other. How we treat each other. What we say about each other. We need to recognize it in the other members of the body and treat them with NO less respect than you would give Jesus Himself.

The question needs to be asked, are you yourself walking in the anointing and are you so full of the spirit of God that you sense His presence in the other members of the body of Christ? Are you filled with God to overflowing or are you merely satisfied to be a Christian period, just living a good moral life. You don't drink, you don't smoke, you don't cuss. Well the Pharisees and the Sadducees didn't drink, or smoke or cuss. That is not the state in which God wants you to live. He wants you to hunger and thirst after Him and seek His face and seek more of His presence in your life. He wants to permeate your whole being so that His glory will radiate from you.

God has an agenda and that is for us to take His glory to some soul that is living in darkness. Jesus, who is the Light of this world, said that we, His followers, are to be lights in this world and that we are to let our light so shine before men that it will cause them to glorify the Father which is in heaven. Realize that Jesus is not only living in you, but wants to shine through you.

~ 20 ~

If You've Heard This Message,

...You Will See My Point

I can talk at 70 miles per hour with gusts of up to 100. I can type even faster. Either way, I have a lot to say. Every where. All the time. To everyone. I just can't talk fast enough, especially when I am relating all that God has done in my life. I want people to see that life is wonderful and special and precious and meaningful. Does that mean I have no problems? Depends on how you look at it.

One day I met my match, a motor mouth named Penny. She was a trainee at my new job, and my unusual license plate caught her attention so she stopped to enquire as to what it meant. Not wanting to miss any opportunity, I recited most of Psalm 40; *"He lifted me up, out of the miry clay, out of the horrible pit and set my feet upon a rock, and established my goings. And He hath put a new song in my mouth, even praise unto our God: many shall see what He has done for me and put their trust in Him".* She then asked if she could ride with me during our training segment because she wanted to hear more. Three days later Penny was sobbing, "Stop the car! Stop the car! I want to give my life to Jesus, NOW!", obviously deeply convicted by the Word of God. Meanwhile, I'm driving up one street and down the other trying to find at least a nice tree to park under, because I wanted her memory of this special life changing event to be more than a dismal scene in a parking spot, in front of a cement wall, at a plaza.

Six years later, Penny is still like a breath of fresh air, telling everyone, everywhere, at every opportunity, about this abundant life that she has discovered. Does that mean she has no problems? Depends on how you look at it.

If you are thinking, "Great, but you don't know the cross I've had to bear. You don't understand my pain and suffering." You are right, I don't. But God does and He says in John 10:10 that it was the devil that came to kill and steal and destroy but Jesus came that you might have life and have it more abundantly. He promises to deliver you out of ALL your afflictions and to give you joy and peace and to bring purpose and meaning to your life. He promises to make your yoke easy and your burden light. Does that mean you will have no problems? Depends on how you look at it.

I would like you to look at someone who's problems I am certain superseded anything you or I will ever have to endure and yet she said, "It's not what happens to you in life that matters, but what you do with it that counts." Her name is Helen Keller. A fever caused her to loose her sight and her hearing when she was 19 months old. Up until the age of seven she behaved like a wild, untamed animal until Alexander Graham Bell introduced her parents to Anne Sullivan who became her live-in teacher and tutor.

Anne's first hurdle was to teach this uncontrollable child obedience before she could begin to teach her finger spell patterns. Teaching her W-A-T-E-R was meaningless until after Helen's hand was placed in a well so that she could connect and realize the association between the finger spelled word and the liquid. The realization then brought thirst for more understanding for the name of each and every object in her dark world. She then learned the shapes of letters. Her marvelous retention earned her the nickname of 'Miracle Child'.

She progressed to reading lips using her fingers and then developed her speech by placing her fingers inside her instructor's mouth to feel the position of the tongue until she learned letters and sounds. This took her many painstaking years, but it shows that through perseverance, excellence can be achieved.

Despite all her disabilities, she was noted as being kind and generous and for having a gift for bringing out the best in other people. It is no surprise that she had numerous friends She had much empathy for the poor and the disabled, yet she declared, "The only true disability is the disability of the heart".

Because her main vehicle of communication to the world was writing, she wrote volumes. Obviously, she had much to say. Her life's work was giving speeches and raising funds for the American Foundation for the Blind. She travelled the world, visited the Queen and even visited disabled soldiers during World War II. She was often seen talking to herself with her fingers which were her windows to the world. I choose to believe that at those times she was talking to God, thanking Him for His many blessings.

Her pearls of wisdom include the statement, "all my life I have tried to avoid ruts such as leaning on the crutches of other people's opinion or losing my childhood sense of wonderment.'

She died peacefully in 1968, at the age of 88, while taking a nap.

Was Helen Keller's life wonderful and special and precious and meaningful? Depends on how you look at it.

~ 21 ~
Why Should I Let Physics Mess Up My Faith

Most people have probably not paid too much attention to the story in 2 Kings chapter 6 where the prophet Elisha threw a stick into the river and an axhead floated to the surface of the water. The simple logistics being that a young seminary student, losing the ax in the river, was very distressed because it was borrowed and sought help from the prophet who sought help from God. God then simply and divinely transcended His laws of gravity and physics and graciously answered the prayer. Without much fanfare or hoopla, the axhead rose to the surface of the water.

That story got my attention. It penetrated my heart and soul and spirit. That is why when I was a young, naive, and a very on-fire-for-God Christian, I had no problem believing any of these scriptures. I prayed for the sick and they recovered. That was not very radical and quite respectable and even accepted that God would and could heal the sick. But the trouble arose when I began to pray for things such as my busted washing machine. I had three teenagers, and after three weeks the blue jeans were meeting me at the front door. The electrician couldn't repair it so my only recourse was to turn to God for help. My most incredulous prayer was over a broken down car whose engine required $2,900 in repairs. Since my total net worth amounted to a little more than zilch, guess what I did instead. Yup, I really did. Just like a little kid, who brings her broken toy to her dad to fix, it never even crossed my mind that my Heavenly Father couldn't or wouldn't help.

Now I don't have to tell you that some older, more 'mature' saints of God look at you like all your ducks are not in a row. They insist that God is too sanctimonious to bother with such temporal issues. They suggested that my feet needed to be firmly planted on the ground. The fact that God did fix these things was of no consequence. So naturally, over the years, wishing to show progression towards spiritual maturity, I slowly and gradually began my descent towards earth. I came to the place where it never even occurred to me to pray these absurdities.

But, thank God, I turned to His Word, rather than the opinions of men and He rekindled the fire that ignited my faith again. I followed God's advice and mounted up on wings as an eagle and began to soar. I discovered that those magnificent birds had continual opposition from crows which attack and peck at their feet as they fly. That eagle just spreads it's wings and soars to an altitude that those crows can't reach. So each year I soar higher and higher. I refuse to cruise where the crows can mess up my faith!

So, three weeks ago when my watch broke, I naturally asked God to fix it and then set the hands at the right time. A few hours later I looked at the time and the hands hadn't moved. I prayed again. Nothing happened. The next day I prayed again reminding God that the money spent to fix this watch could be given to a good cause. Why should I spend money on repairs or on buying a new watch when I already had a watch and a God that was able to make it run. Hoping He saw my logic, I set it at 4:00 o'clock. This continued for days until I finally decided I should be realistic and just go and get a new battery. The jeweller installed it at no charge. I checked the time a few hours later and was more than surprised to find that the hands had not moved. This watch was definitely broken.

Again, I petitioned God, only now I was really serious. I remembered the acronym P.U.S.H. Pray Until Something Happens. I was not going to be deterred. I was going to pray and not stop until it was fixed. Just as simple as that because I am convinced that God honors faith, especially childlike faith that does not doubt or question or predetermine that something is impossible. If faith moves the hands of God, I certainly had enough to move the hands of this watch. I could not accept the fact that I had prayed so fervently for 14 days and that my watch was still stopped. I placed my hand over it and said, "Dear Lord, I stand on your Word that says that You shall supply all of my needs and dear Lord, I need to know what time it is!" That happened over a week ago and my watch has not missed one second since. My faith has gone into orbit!

For those that don't believe it, I say, 'That's why it happens to me and not to you!" Because I do believe. I believe in the God that makes axheads float; therefor I know He can heal your body, restore your marriage and mend your broken heart. But, you need to: Pray Until Something Happens.

~ 22 ~

I Can Hear the Sound of the Abundance of Rain

God is the same, yesterday, today and forever. Aren't you glad? It would be terrible to read of the wondrous things that He has done for His people in the past, and yet to have Him silent and hidden today.

Although, as long as we have His Word, He can not be hidden because His Word is a revelation of Himself. Also, Psalm 19 says that 'the heavens declare the glory of God; and the firmament sheweth His handiwork´. But, I can not help but get discombobulated when He actually appears. One example in the Old Testament was the 'burning bush' which appeared to Moses and was not consumed. Another was the fourth man that appeared in the fiery furnace with Shadrach, Meshach and Abednego. Another theophany (meaning God appearing in a physical form) was the pillar of fire by night and the cloud by day which preceded the Israelites on their journey through the desert during the entire forty years.

It is this cloud that I want to speak about today. God was showing the Israelites, and assuring them, that He was with them on their journey to the Promised Land. Another incident happened when Solomon's Temple was completed. It says, *'that the house was filled with a cloud, even the house of the Lord; so that the priests could not stand to minister by reason of the cloud; for the glory of the Lord had filled the house of God.'*

Today, thousands of years later, God's cloud again manifests where God's people gather to worship Him. I have had it occur in two of my meetings. The first time was last spring, in

Louisiana. Two ladies from the congregation stood up and stated that they could not see me while I was preaching because the cloud of glory was so thick around the altar. Many just came and we fell on our faces and lay prostrate on the platform, bowing in the awesome presence of God, in humble recognition of a very holy moment.

This past summer, in Canada, I held a healing crusade and seminar in the most insignificant and obscure place. Fifty of us met in a large barn that was converted into a church setting. I reminded those present that Jesus was born in a stable. Over the period of two days, the cloud of God's glory appeared four times. I, myself, had the honor and undeserved privilege of seeing it envelop the musicians as they lead us in praise and worship.

Some said it was like a mist. Others thought that something had caught on fire. We all knew that we had met with God as people were gloriously healed. Some had been wracked with pain since the 70's. One lady left her walker. Another's broken wrist was healed. God moved among us in a most powerful way.

The book of Joel talks about the latter rain. That God will pour down His Spirit upon us even more powerfully than in the days of old. This is being evidenced today all over the world. We are living in exciting times. Is the soil of our heart ready to receive the downpour?

The prophet Hosea tells us to break up the fallow ground of our heart so it is no longer stoney and hard and to 'sow to yourselves in righteousness, reap in mercy; for it is time to seek the Lord, till He come and rain righteousness upon you.'

At one point in Exodus, as Aaron was speaking to the congregation, and just before the Lord sent them manna from heaven, it says, *'the Glory of the Lord appeared in the cloud'*. Can we handle the glory of God? Are we ready to receive it?

~ 23 ~

No Apology On This Menu, Just Some Humble Pie

Wanting to give credit where credit was due, I started to tell the pastor how much Barbara had assisted with a particular nine month project, in case he was not aware. Realizing there were another 300 people who also wanted to interact with him about some intricacies from their daily lives, I kept it brief. Too brief I'm afraid because Barbara abruptly snapped, "I did a lot more than that!" I just about fell out of my pew and pastor Fred jolted backwards as if he'd just come upon a rattlesnake.

Driving home I'm thinking, 'this woman is definitely deluded'. She only helped for about one hour a night for six nights and now she's looking for accolades. What nerve! What an aberration! I was furious. I figured furious was an acceptable Christian trait as long as I was ranting in the King James Version. My blood pressure rose higher and higher as I rehashed what I could have said in retaliation when the Lord suddenly interrupted this episode of ungodly rage with two most startling words, "Go apologize"

I almost drove into a tree. I was certain I had heard wrong. This was surely a mistake. God would not be asking such a thing. Even though I came up with argument after argument and some great defense, for some inexplicable reason, God would not reconsider.

More than perplexed, I nonetheless drove to God's destination hoping all the way that God had arranged it so that when I got to her house she would fall at my feet and beg for my forgiveness. Anything's possible!

Upon opening the door, she folded her arms in front of her and stated matter of factly, "I prayed God would convict you." I almost dropped dead. If God was supposed to convict ME, then I must be the one that's in the wrong.

I managed to blurt out some sort of an apology and drove off utterly stupefied. "Lord, how can I have so little understanding of You and Your ways to not realize when I'm wrong?", I cried.

"Oh, I didn't say anything about right or wrong" God interjected, "I simply asked you to go apologize. I just asked you to obey. This is not about right or wrong."

As painful as it was for me to apologize, this was a lesson in Christ-likeness and humility. When there is a conflict, we are to humble ourselves, not start a war.

A scripture in Micah reads: *"He hath showed thee, O man, what is good; and what doth the Lord require of thee, but to do justly, and to love mercy, and to walk humbly with thy God.'*

Another in the book of Hebrews say, *"Follow peace with all men, and holiness, without which no man shall see the Lord. Looking diligently lest any man fail of the grace of God; lest any root of bitterness springing up trouble you, and thereby many be defiled."*

This happened many years ago, but I prayed then that if I could learn anything from this experience it would be to forever remain pliable in the Masters hand and asked Him to ensure that I would never become prideful, arrogant or stiff-necked.

Not wanting any bitterness to take root in my life, I sent Barbara a copy of my book and wrote this inscription; *'And God created the heavens and the earth and all the host of them, and the evening and the morning were the sixth day'*. To God, six days is a very long time. Thank you for the six days and nights you spent editing this book."

It felt good. Funny how doing it God's way always feels soooooooo good.

~ 24 ~

When God Sees His Face --- You're Done

Being strongly opposed to Halloween I considered exposing this unholy day and what it represents once again. I wanted to inform people about the origins that have lead to the celebration of Satan's holiday, but I will spare you. I don't want to be redundant either. The only thing I ask is; if you are considering participating in this event, please first obtain total knowledge and a clear understanding of what you are actually embracing and identifying with.

I am certain that the information would alarm you and cause you to reconsider. I would urge you to read my previous article (October 1999) in the Gondolier's archives or on the Internet.

So instead of writing about this gruesome, sinister phenomenon that has overtaken our society, I want to bless your socks off with something more cheery and refreshing -- three men that were thrown into a furnace. I knew that would make you gasp. Just bear with me. I promise you there is nothing to be alarmed about.

First, I would like to share something that beautifully illustrates the third chapter of Malachi where God states; *'And He shall sit as a refiner and purifier of silver.'* A silversmith, who was relating the process of refining silver, was asked if he had to sit and wait for the silver to be refined or could he go about his business. His reply was that his eye had to be steadily fixed on the furnace because if the time necessary for refining should be exceeded in the slightest degree, the silver would be injured.

God in His wisdom sometimes allows His children to go through the furnace of difficulties so that the dross will be removed from our lives. But while they are being refined by the fiery trial, His eye is steadily intent on the work of purifying, guarding that they not be consumed. He will not let us be tested beyond what we can endure.

If you reflect on some of the hardships that you have had to endure during the course of your life, it will become apparent that those very same events formed the richest quality of your character and personality. Priorities changed and your understanding of what is truly important, valuable and precious in life, quickly rose to the surface.

The silversmith was also asked how he knew the refining process was complete. "Why, that is quite simple," he replied, "when I can see my own image in the silver, the refining process is finished."

Scripture says that by beholding the glory of God, we become as mirrors that brightly reflect His glory. As the Spirit of the Lord works within us, we become more and more like Him.

We need to guard against anything that would spot or tarnish that mirror in us.

Shadrach, Meshach and Abednego were thrown into a furnace, not to be purged but to be destroyed, because they would not bow down and worship a golden image. It was not just a custom but became the command. They answered, *"If it be so, our God whom we serve is able to deliver us from the burning fiery furnace, but if not, be it known unto thee, O king, that we will not serve thy gods, nor worship the golden image which thou hast set up." Into the furnace they go, but Glory to God, the king was astounded when he saw 'a fourth man loose, walking in the midst of the fire, and the form of the fourth man was like the Son of God.'*

They would not compromise, therefore God marvelously honored their integrity and sent His Son to rescue them.

God also sent His Son 2,000 years ago to rescue us from the flames of hell. Not a very popular concept in the 21st century but a very real place nevertheless. The only prerequisite is that we bow our knee to Him. The prophet Joel says in chapter two; *'whosoever calls upon the name of the Lord shall be delivered.'*

~ 25 ~

A Proven Remedy and a Sure Cure -- Son-Shine

The months of January and February are supposed to be the coldest, darkest and bleakest of the entire year. Please notice that I said supposed to be. I can somewhat fathom this stance for those living north of these tropical orange groves, but for those people here in this sun-soaked paradise, I am positive that it is a state of mind. And I am going to refer you to my sponsor to prove my point. Proverbs 17:22 says, *"a merry heart doeth good like a medicine, but a broken spirit drieth the bones."* In other words, a broken spirit makes one sick.

I am not a doctor, but I guarantee that our attitudes and our outlook have a dramatic effect on our physical well being. Our physical, emotional and spiritual lives are intertwined. Stress is proven to cause diabetes and a long list of other illnesses. Worry and anxiety cause ulcers. Depression and sadness weaken our immune system and make us susceptible to almost everything else.

Psalm 118 says, *"this is the day which the Lord hath made, we will rejoice and be glad in it"*. Before I expound on this scripture, let me just say that there are two things that I know for a fact: there is a God and I am not Him -- but I would like to add a word to this passage nevertheless and that word is 'choose'. When I get up in the morning, and the world is not as I would expect or have anticipated, I can react by becoming a toxic person, creating a toxic waste dump environment around me, or I can quote, "'this is the day which the Lord hath made, I will

CHOOSE to rejoice and be glad in it." I'm determined not to respond negatively to my circumstances.

Where did I learn this tremendous life-enhancing lesson? In God's instruction manual, of course. He gave us His inspired Word so that our lives could be rich and full, plus productive and gloriously meaningful. The best example being King David. When he came back after fighting the Philistines, they discovered that the Amalekites had raided the city, burned it to the ground and carried off all the women and children. David's soldiers were so distraught that they began turning against him and started talking of killing him.

Sometimes, as in David's situation, when we are trying to do all that we know how, and especially when we are attempting to do much for God, those around us, those closest to us, instead of encouraging us, become our greatest obstacles. We can give up. We can give in. Or we can instead do as David did: 'he encouraged himself in the Lord'

This conveys that he gained inner strength, plus boldness and courage. These things spring up from inside because of knowing God. Knowing who He is and what He has done for us. As David turned to the Lord, put on the ephod and inquired of Him, a powerful anointing came on him which enabled David and his men to chase after their enemy and to get back what had been stolen from them.

Are we going to let Satan, the enemy of our soul, rob and steal and destroy even one precious day from our life, or are we going to decisively encourage ourselves in the Lord and become like an artesian well, so full of the Spirit and anointing of God that we splash and gush joy on all those that come into our presence?

On three occasions Jesus made the statement, *"be of good cheer"*. He said, *"be of good cheer, thy sins are forgiven"*. Meaning, we are heaven-bound. A tremendous reason, I would say, to 'be glad'.

Another time, when His disciples were frightened and troubled He said, *"Be of good cheer, it is I, Jesus!"* I, Jesus, your Creator, your Savior; your Redeemer and your Lord. Your Provider, your Defender, your Shield and your Buckler. I, Jesus, your Guide and your Peace. Your Comforter and your Heavenly Father. Attributes that enable us to face any obstacle.

Lastly,*"Be of good cheer, I,* (Jesus) *have overcome the world!"* Let Him, the bright Morning Star arise in your hearts.

~ 26 ~

It's Never a Mistake When You Listen to God's Prompt

A funny thing happened to me on the way to Kentucky. I was scheduled to do a three day seminar at a local church which would provide for our accommodations during those three days. My next stop, Atlanta, was 12 days away. We needed a place to stay until then so I called a lady whom I knew and asked if my husband and I could stay with her. She said, "Sure, come on down." Three days after we arrived she moved away!!!

Oh, of course, she brought us along, but there still happened to be a major problem. She was moving from a furnished house to an unfurnished one. This meant we had no table, no chairs, no t.v., no shower and no bed. Not even a telephone.

I learned a long time ago to travel with an air mattress, but I could not see us laying around the house, on our backs, all day long, for nine extra days.

When we travel to Mexico, I pray for indoor plumbing and hope the Lord realizes that air conditioning at my age is NOT a luxury but a life-sustaining necessity. But this was Kentucky! A phone and a chair, I consider absolutely mandatory! My first impulse was to head for 'dem thar hills' except that we would then have to stay in a hotel and that was not anywhere on our budget.

I was certain I had missed God! Especially since the remainder of my six week trip consisted of many more three and four day gaps apparently devoid of purpose. Had I truly allowed God to plan my itinerary?

Apparently I did. As furniture and other modern conveniences arrived intermittently, those 12 days, which appeared a colossal mistake, turned out to be the fullest, richest and most rewarding experience that I will treasure for a very long time to come. Our days were filled with divine appointments waiting at every turn. Something that can not occur when I zoom from one engagement to another. My other stops also held wonderfully delightful surprises. Literally dozens of additional people were touched by God and their lives eternally changed, all because I had the extra time and space to allow God to move in His way and in His timing.

Why is it that we doubt God has orchestrated the circumstances as soon as they don´t seem to unfold according to our specifications? We have such finite vision. We need a paradigm shift. It is God and only God that sees the whole picture.

To better illustrate my point I want to share the story of the mountain climber, who after years of preparation, decided to conquer the Aconcagua alone. As he was climbing a ridge, night fell, visibility became zero and he lost his footing and he slipped and fell. Falling rapidly, his life flashed before his eyes. He was certain he would die but moments later he was jolted to a full stop which almost tore him in half. He then remembered, that as he was trained to do, he had staked himself with a long rope tied to his waist. Suspended and dangling in the air he screamed, "GOD, HELP ME, PLEASE GOD, HELP ME!"

God replied, "Of course I will. Cut the rope."

At this point I think I would have asked, "Is there anybody else up there?"

The terrified climber clutched the rope even tighter. The next day the rescue team found him frozen to death, hanging strongly secured to the rope .... TWO FEET OFF THE GROUND.

Do you place your trust in your rope and your plans, or do you trust God?

'For I know the plans that I have for you sayeth the Lord. They are plans for good and not for evil, to give you a future and a hope. Then shall you call upon me, and you shall go and pray unto me, and I will hearken unto you. And you shall seek me, and find me, when you shall search for me with all your heart."

If you pray and then obey His leading you can enter this New Year confident that God has your best interests at heart and that He is directing your every step.

~ 27 ~
Why Am I Sitting Here When I Could Be Getting Rich?

Since I practically promised you that I would make this month's article entertaining, I am going to endeavor somehow to take the sting out of yet another biblical character being struck dead by God because of disobedience.

During a real estate slump in the mid-eighties, I was assigned to sell five houses in a New Home Subdivision. I sat in this vacant house month after month. Not a creature was stirring, not even a mouse, much less a buyer. It looked like I would never sell that house.

I kept asking God if I could either stay home or go back to the resale market which was at least nominally selling. He simply said, "No."

One day my friend Suzie called saying all the purchasers were making a run on the resale homes. She was making money hand over fist. Although it sounded very appealing, I relayed how just that very day God had shown me to stay put and not go anywhere.

Major confusion developed when just a couple of hours later another friend, who does not even know Suzie, called saying that I just had to come back to Montreal Trust because the market was booming. She would not accept that God would have me go to work every day, eight hours a day, five days a week and not make a red cent. She was convinced I was getting my wires crossed and expected to see me at my old desk the very next morning.

God is not the author of confusion and He is certainly not slack concerning compensation for those out there working for a living, so I determined to persuade Him to let me go and make my fortune.

To my astonishment, He did not budge and when I questioned Him on the unparalleled coincidence of two unrelated people calling on the exact same day with the exact same advice, He merely pointed me to the story in 1 Kings chapter 13 where the Lord told a prophet from Judah to go into a city and prophesy to the king. While he was there, he was neither to eat nor drink any water nor to return to Judah by the same road by which he came.

As he was returning by way of Bethel, an old prophet caught up to him and invited him to his home for a meal saying, *"I am a prophet too and an angel gave me a message from the Lord. I am to take you home with me and give you some food and water."* *"But,"* scripture records, *"he lied."*

Unfortunately the younger prophet followed him home and ate some food and drank some water. While they were still sitting at the table a message from the Lord came saying that because he had disobeyed God's clear command when he was told not to have anything to eat or drink, that his carcass would not be buried in the grave of his fathers'. To make a very long story short, on his way out of town, a lion attacked and killed him.

This story is self-explanatory. You can jump to any conclusions you like and form your own opinions after you go and read the whole story in your bibles, but let me tell you, that after reading that passage, there was not the slightest chance that I was going to leave my "divinely appointed and allocated station in life." Not for the next million years. If I never made another nickel, I was going to keep showing up, same time, same place, same empty house.

Less than a month later, the Lord released me to go back into the resale market and I made an incredible amount of money in a very short period of time which more than compensated for the nine months of leanness and lack.

And that, coincidentally enough, was only after my autobiography ʹUphill Climbʹ was written and completed because I had those many quiet hours, without any disturbance, without distraction, day after day, month after month. Something that could not possibly have transpired had I been anywhere else, not even at home, because I had three teenagers, a husband on shift work and the demands of caring for a large home. The peaceful hours I needed to hear His direction and His leading could only be achieved at this secluded heaven where I raised my Ebenezer, a memorial of Godʹs great deliverance and help throughout my life. Certainly and clearly a better testimony than being eaten alive by a lion.

~ 28 ~
God is Talking --- Is Your Heart Listening?

Sometimes people separate the God of the bible, that God of soooo long ago, from the God of the 21st century. But that very same Book, also referred to as the 'Basic Instructions Before Leaving Earth', states that He is the same yesterday, today and forever. He never changes. He is the one constant in the universe. As a matter of fact, it alone is the rule and guide that portrays the character, the nature and the heart of God. Though many contest and challenge this fact today, I am convinced that God would not leave us down here to fend for ourselves nor expect us to exist on this planet on a hit and miss basis, never knowing or determining His mind and will for our lives.

Most believers are comfortable with this statement, but can really get out of joint when told that He also speaks to us directly. I can't imagine why. When the prophet Samuel was just a little boy, the Lord called him by name three times and Samuel replied, *"Here am I"* and the rest is history. God worked mightily through Samuel for the rest of his life because Samuel was willing to be one thing, God's servant.

My mother said that since the time I was just a little more than two years old, I could not pass by a church without insisting I needed to go inside because God was calling my name. She said I would lay down on the ground and kick up such a fuss that they had no choice but to let me go and stick my head through the doors. Just taking a peek seemed to satisfy me, I didn't actually need to go all the way in.

The first time Moses heard the voice of God he was out in the desert, content to be minding the flocks, happy he wasn't in jail for murder, until he came upon a burning bush. He decided to investigate why the bush was not being consumed when a voice from inside the bush called out his name, *"Moses, Moses"* and Moses responded, *"Here am I"*. Chapter after chapter we see this very humble, elderly man, with a speech impediment yet, talking to God on a regular basis.

I grew up hoping that there was a God while society tried to convince me that He was a myth for the unsophisticated and uneducated. And then one day, He spoke to me audibly and told me that I was going to have twin boys eighteen months before they were born. Throughout my pregnancy my doctor insisted that I was going to have only one child and that I was setting myself up for disappointment. My family and friends thought I must have hallucinated. God proved everyone wrong. My twin boys arrived according to His word

God spoke continuously to everyone, everywhere, all the time but my final example is a most unlikely candidate. He hated the Christian faith and persecuted Christians without mercy until suddenly on the road to Damascus a light from heaven shined around about him and he heard a voice saying, *"Saul, Saul, why do you persecute me?"* He surrendered his life right there and then to Jesus Christ and went on to become the Apostle Paul who wrote most of the New Testament.

I almost dare not tell you that I ran smack into God one day on my bike. I'll save that story for another time. It might just be too much for you to handle at one sitting but this all happen before I had ever read a page of the bible or heard any of these similar instances.

The Apostle John records, "The sheep hear His voice and He calleth His own sheep by name and leadeth them out. He goeth before them and the sheep follow Him, for they know His voice."

His sheep hear His voice. It is nothing unusual. It is the norm. Sometimes it is through the pages of scripture. Sometimes it is audible. Daily He speaks to our heart. Is your heart listening?

Jesus Himself confirms, *"Behold, I stand at the door* (of your heart) *and knock, if any man hear my voice and open the door, I will come in to him and will fellowship with him."* He desires a relationship with you. To have a relationship it is necessary to communicate. Imperative actually, but first, go answer the door!

~ 29 ~

A New Twist On The Twenty-third Psalm

Robert Ketchum tells of a Sunday School teacher who asked a group of children if anyone could quote the entire Twenty-third Psalm. A golden haired four-and-a-half year old raised her hand. A bit skeptical, the teacher had her come to the front of the class. The little girl made a perky little bow, and said, "The Lord is my Shepherd, that's all I want." She bowed again and sat down. What a marvelous interpretation!

Wouldn't it be awesome if we could remain as idealistic as that small content child? Scripture ensures that we not only can, but advises we must, to receive abundant life.

Is this hard to believe and accept? It used to be for me. Even though I truly believed, all the way down to my toes, that 'because' the Lord was my Shepherd, I would not have lack, there was a limit to even my faith. Especially since my life radically changed back in 1991 when my husband and I were embezzled and therefore lost everything we owned. Our lives radically changed because the related circumstances led to our income being reduced permanently by about 75%. We needed to learn in a hurry how to live without a great deal of stuff. Especially the bells, the whistles and the perks.

I must be a slow learner because it did not take very long to max out one credit card, and then another and another. I'm ashamed to say I became panic-stricken, then tormented. Where was it going to end? The enormous faith I had prior to this turn of events, flew right out the window. Sadly, I lost all hope. I was certain we were going to suffer lack in spite of the fact that my

Shepherd promised to supernaturally provide for me, just as He clothes the lilies of the field and feeds the birds of the air.

I recalled a story about a devout Quaker who leaned on his fence one day and watched a new neighbor move in next door. After all kinds of modern appliances, electronic gadgets, plush furniture and costly wall hangings had been carried in, the onlooker called over the fence, " If you find you're lacking anything neighbor, let me know and I'll show you how to live without it."

You can live without a lot of things, but you cannot live without hope. Eventually, we maxed out our sixth credit card. I became hysterical and called my good friend Sue. She asked me why I didn't listen to my own advise and reminded me of what I had told her twenty years ago when she was going to apply for a credit card. I had said that God was her Provider, not Master Card nor Visa nor anything else and that all she needed to do was trust Him. This is why, 20 years later, after raising two kids on her own, she owed no man anything.

Definitely an easier sermon to preach than to live, but I did not have much choice, so very hesitantly I agreed to put away the credit cards and put God's word to the test. I've never looked back! The Lord provides supernaturally, again and again and again. Miraculously. Not just my every need but the very desires of my heart.

Let me tell you the latest. A friend came to church, looking radiant and much slimmer in an exquisite, new, cranberry-red outfit. She said, "The sale ends today, get over to the mall."

Not having any cash on hand, I started to negotiate with God, especially since cranberry-red was my favorite color and since I certainly needed to look slimmer. I reminded Him how many years I had gone without using my credit card and also how big a dent I had made in my debt. He reminded me of my commitment. I concluded that I would have to remain true to my word and continue to live according to God's precepts and leave the outcome in His hands. If I didn't have the money, I would not go near the mall.

Just hours later, this same friend Annette invited us to her house for dinner. She took me to her closet and presented me with five very expensive, very spectacular designer dresses. Two of them were cranberry-red! My way, I would have one lovely dress, His way, I had five.

When He becomes all we want, and His will becomes our ultimate desire, we end up with everything else. *"Seek ye first the Kingdom of God and His righteousness and all these things shall be added unto you."*

~ 30 ~

Just a Little Spark Can Set Your Life Ablaze

Are you one of those people who do not see God's plan or purpose for your life any more? Have you simply been coasting for years, convinced that God has bypassed you somehow? Has your enthusiasm and excitement faded and your light become dim? It is probably some past disappointment that is responsible. Or maybe a temporary setback has brought serious discouragement that has unleashed utter hopelessness and snuffed out the zeal you once possessed.

Do not fret, because neither can prevent you from becoming all that God wants you to be. You have not burned out. Your greatest hour is yet to come. You better trim your wick.

One reason that I am so certain is because of my own personal experience and the other is because of the bamboo tree. "What possible connection does a bamboo tree have with my condition?" you ask. Everything! You'll see!

You will find that if you plant a bamboo tree and you fertilize it and water it day after day and month after month that absolutely nothing happens. The next year you add more fertilizer and more water and still nothing happens. The third year you give it more of this and more of that and for all your effort you just get more disappointment. By the fourth year you are convinced that you've planted a dud. The fifth year is no different from those previous unproductive years and you want to pull it out by it's roots.

Do not fret and do not give up because what happens is that at the end of the fifth year that bamboo tree grows 45 feet in a matter of 30 days. All that water, all that fertilizer, all that sunshine was being assimilated, was being absorbed and stored up for the day of exploit.

Do not let the past affect your present. Simply learn from the past. Absorb the lessons and then move into your divine appointment. Forget your mistakes and your failures. Forget the years that seemed unproductive. Forget the people that have said, 'This must be God's will for your life -- to remain stunted.' Don't give place to that kind of faith-destroying mentality. The enemy of your soul wants you to believe that you are going to live a mediocre, going nowhere, doing nothing existence and that you have come to the end of the road. That is just not a fact for anyone that is a child of God's.

After I had been on roller skates for God for over ten years, my wheels suddenly screeched to a complete halt. I spent the next three and one half years believing that I had lost the favor of God in my life and that for some reason God changed His mind and pulled me out of His service. I lost all hope. You can live without an awful lot of things, but you cannot live without hope. I wanted to die.

Suddenly, the Lord sent me a messenger to tell me it was all a lie and that the devil had very subtly and systematically convinced me that the game plan had changed. My simple proclamation, "Get thee behind me satan", ended my many years of torment because I had received revelation knowledge of the power of God behind those words. Yet, for another year and a half I walked around in a daze, licking my wounds, recuperating from the onslaught until God sent another messenger asking, "What are you doing hiding in the cave Mrs. Elijah? Come out of that cave and run with the message." That mere insight of my self-imposed restrictions and the affirmation of God's decree for my life re-ignited my fire. I've never looked back.

I'm certain that after Joseph was sold into slavery by his brothers and during his 12 years in exile it looked like God's plan for his life was merely a pipe dream. Especially during the two years when he was cast into a dungeon for something he didn't even do. But God had a mighty call on Joseph's life. He was made Governor of all of Egypt. He preserved his entire family and all of Egypt during the years of famine.

Moses hid in the desert 40 years until God commissioned him to go and set the captives free and lead them into the Promised Land.

It doesn't matter if you have been in the desert for 40 days or 40 years, God has a divine call for you to fulfill. I bring you the message that God has set you as a *'beacon upon the top of a hill'*.

~ 31 ~
An Ounce of Humor Accomplishes More Than a Pound of Wrath

How would you respond to rebuke? Or criticism? Or any negative attack that is directed at you personally and requires a response? It is certainly a precarious situation to be in. Especially if you are hosting a live television program. You are completely defenseless and vulnerable, not knowing who or what might come at you next. Taking telephone calls on the air, while being broadcast live over satellite to an entire nation causes me just a "little bit" of trepidation. Never- the-less, I sit there week after week staring at a little red dot in the middle of the camera completely dependent upon God and reasonably confident that He will not let me embarrass myself (or Him).

The majority of the viewers and callers are most encouraging and shower me with love. But then, there is that 'one'. There is ALWAYS one. One that is determined to pull you down, knock you out and be the very instrument that keeps you humble and on your toes.

Fortunately for me, this viewer chose to e-mail me rather than humiliate me on the air. He basically wrote that he was a Christian, studying anthropology at University and stated that after watching me a dozen times, saw that the Bible, which was only intended to be a quasi-structure tool, seemed to completely control me instead. That meant that I was abandoning my free will and this was therefore a great handicap.

GLORY TO GOD -- to be criticized because my life is centered around the Word of God and to be lambasted because I use it as the final and ultimate authority regarding any and all issues is the greatest compliment I could receive. Still I got a bit out of joint because this man's intent was not to bless but to find fault. Plus, I read this e-mail at the end of the program, in the middle of the night, at which point I had been awake for over 24 hours. I was liable to say something I might regret so I prayed for God's wisdom.

God has a most wonderful sense of humor. Instead of reproof, He had me write this analogy: "as with a car manual, you don't read it and then apply only the parts that suit your ideas and purposes if you want your car to run efficiently. You either accept the 'whole' counsel of God, or have the car sitting in your driveway, or on the side of the road, missing gas, missing oil or just with rusty spark plugs. It could be that you didn't know how your windshield wipers work so you have stayed home every time it rains or snows, therefore spending half your life immobile. To then say that the car manual controls your life because it shows you where the switch to turn the wipers is located or shows you how to release the gas cap, or when to replace the spark plugs is a bit absurd. Simply put, if you operate your car according to the MANUFACTURER'S manual, you will have an efficient and useful vehicle allowing for a pleasant journey. Disregard the instructions and you will possibly be going nowhere, doing nothing very quickly.

There are thousands of people out there whose cars have no gas, no oil, and dead batteries and God has simply called me to point them to the MANUAL and send them to the MECHANIC so that they can have a pleasant journey and end up at the right destination, not in the ditch.

For those that don't have a car, don't want a car and would just rather walk, I suggest you don't ignore the road signs, such as 'Danger - High Voltage' or 'One Way' or 'Detour'. They are not meant to control you, just warn you of what lies ahead. Obviously, they have information which you don't. Plus, if you're out walking in the dark and you run into someone that says, "Look out, you're about to walk off that steep cliff", you might consider going to get a flash light and checking it out, instead of blindly or stubbornly continuing to race toward destruction. But then again, the choice is yours, you don't have to. It's just a suggestion."

I know I was not the author of those words because I'm just not into cars and I was not even remotely amused by this person's slam. Thankfully God's character surfaced rather than my own. God's *'soft answer turneth away wrath'*. Two weeks later this same man wrote and said that my response caused him to take a serious look at God's Word and he has now started a Bible Studies Course so that he can have a better knowledge of the bible. I am so glad God doesn't let me mess up --- this time anyway.

~ 32 ~

God Will Send Fire From Heaven

... Or Whatever Else You Decree

One of the most powerful demonstrations of God's answer to prayer was when God sent fire from heaven in response to Elijah's prayer.

The prophet Elijah was sent to confront King Ahab and his wicked wife Jezebel because they promoted the worship of false gods. This king did more to anger the Lord than any of the other kings of Israel before him, so God sent Elijah to proclaim a drought that lasted more than three years. Withholding rain was a little more than befitting because those that worshiped Baal believed he was the god who brought the rains and the bountiful harvests, so God decided to show them "who" was in charge of that department and of everything else for that matter.

The Lord commanded Elijah to bring all the people to Mount Carmel, along with the 850 false prophets so that the people would stop wavering between two opinions and start following the one and only true God.

Because the odds were in their favor, they agreed to prepare two bulls, one for Elijah and one for themselves and laid the pieces on their altars. The false prophets prayed to their gods all morning, afternoon and into the evening. They shouted and danced and even cut themselves with knives but they saw no reply. Elijah then dug a trench three feet wide around his altar and piled wood on it and saturated the bull and the wood with water so that it overflowed and filled the trench. He prayed,

"Lord God, let it be known this day that You are God and that I am your servant and that I have done all this at your word so that this people may turn their hearts back to You again."

This request was not so that the people would bow down and worship Elijah nor was it to promote his ministry. Neither will God honor 'blab it and grab it' theology. God only responds when the motives are pure, the heart is right and the intent is to bring glory and honor to Him..

'Then the fire of the Lord fell and consumed the burnt sacrifice, the wood, the stones and the dust and it licked up all the water that was in the trench.' 1 Kings 18:38

This was an incredibly amazing audio visual display and it obviously produced the right effect because scripture says *"Now when all the people saw it, they fell on their faces and said, 'The Lord, He is God!'"*

Yes, He is and great is the fact that He is the same, *'yesterday, today and forever more'!* We need to know that we can call on heaven to pull down every stronghold in our life and the lives of our loved ones and in our community and throughout the entire world and that God will send fire at OUR word.

Impossible? Not at all! Let me tell you about the night I was praying for a lady who had called the television program I was hosting. In the middle of my prayer, all the fire alarms started to blare and we had to go off the air and evacuate the studio as fire trucks raced toward the building. They soon determined that there was no fire, no danger and no earthly reason for those alarms to sound.

The next morning, David Mainse, the producer and president said, "Donna, you be careful now, ya hear! Don't go burning down my building."

I had no idea of what he meant until I watched a video tape of the program and heard myself praying, "Lord God, I pray that the fire of God comes down........." Ringggg!

Impossible? Not at all! God wants to come and burn out anything and everything in us that is not of Him and He wants to make us 'as fire'. He wants to ignite our spirits and our souls and wants to set us ablaze for Him, manifesting Himself in and through us because fear and uncertainty about the future has gripped the world and people are desperately searching for the true and living God. At the same time there are many false gods vying for their hearts. There- fore we must walk in the supernatural power of God decreeing peace and blessings in these times of peril. We must act and live as the children of God so as to remove all and any doubt so that the people may say, *'The Lord, HE is God!"*

~ 33 ~

Abandon Your Cave ... Move to Higher Ground

Last month I wrote about the prophet Elijah calling down fire from heaven, which happened to be one of the greatest and most dramatic displays of God's power and might in the old testament. Please notice I said God's power and might, not Elijah's. It was also God's power and might that enabled him to then outrun the kings chariot all the way to Jezreel. This 20 mile marathon would be a miracle in itself, but what is most astonishing is that Elijah was 80 years old at the time.

Obviously the hand of God was upon this man, yet here we have Elijah, who upon hearing the threat of one mere mortal female, is fleeing for his life. One woman almost stopped the call of God upon his life. Picture this, ravens are feeding him; the flour and oil doesn't run out; the fire of God falls at his word; he is baked angel food that enables him to travel 200 miles which took 40 days and 40 nights. You would think that after all these tremendous miracles that this mighty prophet of God wouldn't run from Godzilla; yet, here he is hiding in a cave crying, *"Woe is me!"*

It doesn't take much to cause us to run for cover. Our catastrophes are usually custom designed and orchestrated to keep us dormant and ineffective. Satan has had 6,000 years of practice to achieve this goal, knowing exactly how to keep us from reaching our destiny and keep us from walking in our victory. He knows what is going to make us run for the cave and what is going to strike terror into our heart. Often he uses intimidation. Intimidation is very corrosive and damaging. It caused me to sit around doing nothing, going nowhere for years.

It could be fear and anxiety. It could be depression. Know that Jesus has given us the authority to bind those harassing spirits so we can walk in peace and freedom. Be assured that we have been given spiritual weapons to pull down those strongholds. It is not dependent upon who is chasing us, it is dependent on who we are in Him.

Sometimes our caves are self-imposed. Maybe our imperfections are holding us back. Well, God knows our imperfections better than we do, yet He still trusts us with His glory.

Maybe we have failed in some way. Know that God has work for us to do even after we fail. God didn't take the keys back from Peter when he messed up. Instead He changed Peter from glory to glory.

Maybe lies have been told against us. Live so no-one will believe them and go and read Psalm 27 verses 11 to 14.

Maybe it's not Jezebel, but the person beside us in our pew that is causing us grief. Psalm 55 talks about the friend whose words are smoother than butter, but war is in their heart and their words are like daggers.

At those times it is not the past miracles that enable us to stand. When Jezebel seeks our blood, it doesn't matter how many we have seen or what great feat God has performed at our word. The sustaining power of God is entirely His Word and what that Word says about our circumstances. As long as we are embracing God, the anointing does not lift. The mantle of anointing rested upon Elijah even when he pulled out of the race. Nothing had changed between the miracle on Mount Carmel to the cave except Elijah's perception.

The mantle is on our shoulders and the glory of God rests upon us because we belong to Him, even when in the wilderness, even in the cave. We do not need to strive, for out of our belly shall flow rivers of living water because we believe and serve Him who is the Fountain of living Water. We shall never thirst again and it shall be within us a well of water springing up into everlasting life.

One caution, we need to keep the spring of water within our soul pure. Our life has to exalt Jesus. Our words have to uplift Jesus. Our actions have to express God's holiness and righteousness because we are the expression of His voice to this world. So come out of that cave and run with the message!

~ 34 ~

Does An Angel Have To Kick You?

When I first became a Christian I believed that if you professed to be a Christian, you could say no evil, do no evil or think no evil. I also naively believed that I wouldn't find one iota of error in a Charismatic church. God sent an angel to correct me and divert me from disaster.

My friend and I were at a meeting which announced that they were going to start 'Learn How To Heal' classes. This peaked my interest as I had already prayed for many that were sick or in pain and God had wonderfully healed them.

I was suggesting that I could take some time off work and Fiona could get a baby sitter when my body jerked so vigorously that I almost flew off my chair. We were sitting in the very last row and I very abruptly turned to see who would kick me in the middle of a church service, when I heard a voice, though it was not out loud, so clearly and sternly state, "You do not learn to heal, it is a gift from me."

I grabbed Fiona's arm and rambled, "We can't go. We can't go to this. It's a gift! You do not learn to heal, it's a gift from God!"

When I wrote my autobiography I included this incident and was very disturbed to discover that two ladies, who I felt were the pillars of my church, adamantly insist that God does not kick people and that Jesus was meek and mild and just tiptoed around. They had been Christians their entire life and had never heard of such nonsense. Since they were supposed to be my mentors and my role models, I concluded that I had a very serious problem. I needed to find out immediately if I had a supernatural experience or if I was bouncing off walls and possibly psychotic. Especially since I was meeting more and more Christians that had never walked in the supernatural realm that seemed to be a constant in my life.

I had just finished reading a book where the man was so serious about hearing from God that he got on his face on the floor and prayed for seven days and seven nights. I decided I was going to do the same and not get up until I heard from God and He was going to have to explain to my husband when he got home from work what I was doing there on the floor. I needed to know if God was truly the God of the bible or if I should be on medication.

I wasn't there even 10 minutes when God said, (impressed upon me) "Get up, lickety split, get your bible." Well, Glory to God, I just happened to open it at the story where Peter was in jail and the angel came and slapped him and said, "Come on Peter, let's go, we're outta here!" I thought, "If God can send an angel to slap Peter, who am I to tell God He can't send an angel to kick me?"

Those ladies were sincere but they were sincerly wrong. They based their understanding of God solely on what they themselves had experienced or should I say NOT experienced. This unfortunately brings much intimidation and quenches the faith necessary to live our lives led by the Spirit of God. This is why my next encounter with an angel kept me from discloseing what God was speaking to me. As a group of us were praying, the Lord said, "There is an angel, sent from the throne room of God with a special message. Tell them."

I opened one eye and peered around the room and thought, "Nope, I don't see anything, I don't say anything." The Lord repeated the same sentence again. This time I had a sense that he was more than 12 feet tall, jutting (stretching) through the ceiling of the room into the apartment above us. Since I could not prove that there was an angel amongst us, I decided to write the experience down on a piece of paper and wait until I received some sort of confirmation.

Not even a minute later, one of the ladies got up and said, "God just so strongly impressed upon me to read the last chapter of the book of Revelation." She picked up a bible and read, "I Jesus have sent mine angel to testify unto you these things in the churches. I am the root and the offspring of David, and the bright and morning star............Surely I come quickly. Amen. Even so, come, Lord Jesus."

Two thousand years ago angels announced that the babe in the manger is the Savior of the world. Today they are announcing that He is returning soon as the King of Kings and the Lord of Lords to judge the living and the dead. On that day, what will be your fate?

~ 35 ~

Have I Got a Deal For You!

A very long time ago I came to realize that nobody needs my opinion, because opinions are like bellybuttons, everyone has one of their own. Yet, anybody that knows me, sees me on television or reads anything that I have penned, realizes very quickly that I am very opinionated. I wear this characteristic as a badge of honor and boldly state my opinions everywhere, all the time, to everyone.

One good example is when I used to declare that I was a very good salesperson when I was in real estate. It was NOT an opinion. It was NOT pride. It was merely a fact and I will explain why. I was a topnotch salesperson because I never attempted to sell refrigerators to Eskimos. A good con artist will attempt to do that. Only someone very unscrupulous would try to persuade you to part with your hard-earned money for something that you didn't want or need. I was a good and very opinionated salesperson because I believed that the home I was presenting to my clients was the answer to their hopes and dreams. I believed in it's superior construction and quality of workmanship. I knew the property was in the choicest location. It was also affordable. I staked my reputation and good name on the fact that buying this property would be an extremely wise investment for their future. I was convinced beyond a shadow of a doubt that as they signed on the dotted line, they would be so positively affected by this new decision and venture that it would enhance the very quality of their lives.

You can just imagine then how vocal I became when I discovered that Jesus said, *"no man cometh unto the Father, but by me"* and that we can be saved and forgiven and that our names will then be written in the Book of Life? Plus that there is a mansion in heaven being prepared for those that confess with their mouth the Lord Jesus, and believe in their heart that God hath raised Him from the dead. We will then be walking on the streets of gold for all eternity.

Upon discovering *'the Way, the Truth and the Life'* I could not keep it to myself any more than I would hide the fact that I had discovered the cure for cancer. I declare this glorious news with a fiery passion that comes from God Himself.

I got especially excited when I noticed where God asks, 'How then shall they call on Him in whom they have not believed? And how shall they believe in Him of whom they have not heard? And how shall they hear without a preacher?" A preacher? Oh yes, I figured I was going to be a better preacher than I was a real estate agent. A very opinionated preacher because I was quoting the very words of God Himself. Like Jesus, who said, *"I speak to the world those things which I have heard of the Father."* Now, THAT´S opinionated!

He didn't have to say it twice, yet He did: in the first chapter of Jeremiah He said to me and all those that become His, *"I knew you before you were formed in your mother's womb, before you were born I sanctified you and appointed you as my spokesman to the world. For you will go wherever I send you and speak whatever I tell you to. Behold I have put my words in thy mouth to warn the nations and the kingdoms of this world."*

My friend Wendy Sitar in Augusta, Georgia wrote this lovely poem that expresses much better than I have, what I am trying to say:

I Am Not The Author

I am not the author, of the words that pass my way

But only an earthen vessel, being prayerfully lead each day.

Though the words pass from my hand, and may originate from my heart.

Ti's really God's Holy Spirit, who is the author from the start.

So if credit is to be given, please don't give it just to me.

But give it to our Lord above, for He's the author -- not me.

~ 36 ~

A Crown of Glory That Fadeth Not Away

Recently, after experiencing a few very discouraging weeks and becoming quite irritated with people in general, I had the awesome privilege of meeting Cheryl Prewitt Salem, a former Miss America. Our interaction over a three-day period had a very profound and powerful impact on me that quickly changed my mood and totally transformed my outlook.

Was it her captivating beauty that had me transfixed? No, I meet beautiful people every day. Some even prettier.

Was it her title or celebrity status? No, I have never been one to be star-struck. If someone told me that Queen Elizabeth was just a block away, I don't think I could be enticed away from the book I was reading.

Was it her charismatic personality? No. Believe me, I have met both Mr. and Mrs. Personality, only to find they carried more venom than a rattlesnake and I had enough sense to flee for my life. Charm unfortunately can be concocted for each and every occasion and for self-seeking motives and selfish ambitions leaving a trail of broken, hurting people.

Could it have been the fact that she made others feel important? I was told that upon hearing that 'Midnight Cry' had a very special and significant meaning in my life that she then chose to sing it during her television interview the following night. That certainly endeared her to my heart, but no, it was none of the above.

Was it because she didn't drink or smoke or cuss? Not at all. Dead people don't drink or smoke or cuss. The Pharisees and the Sadducees didn't drink or smoke or cuss either and Jesus called this religious crowd a generation of vipers. No, this certainly did not impress Jesus and it was not what impressed me. It was her spirit! She glows. She radiates. There is excitement in her voice. She exudes life. She is like a breath of fresh air. Not because she hasn't had trials and tribulation. Much misfortune has plagued her life and brought great pain and heartbreak her way. Despite a traffic accident which left her with 160 stitches to her face, she pressed on to receive the crown and title of Miss USA. After tragically losing her little six-year-old daughter, despite her grief, she gave hope to others by stating that her daughter was not a memory back in her past, but was in her future, in the arms of Jesus, waiting at the pearly gates. Though she fought a battle with cancer Cheryl is alive and vibrant, living in the power of God. Despite all the devastation in her life, her warmth and kindness makes her a true personification of everything that it means to be a Christian. The powerful anointing surrounding Cheryl is obviously a result of her intense intimacy with Jesus. The amount of time we spend with Him is what makes us more like Him.

I observed Cheryl during a cruel verbal attack, which you could see by her demeanor wounded her deeply, remain sweet and she responded to that malicious slur in a most gracious and dignified manner, in love and humility, with neither malice nor revenge.

I empathized immediately because I recalled once when I came to church sobbing about what had just happened to me and what a terrible impact this would have on my entire family, one of the 'Pharisee crowd' commented, "Well, it's about time something wiped that smile off your face and knocked off those rose-colored glasses." I was probably more shaken and devastated by her comment than by my misfortune, but I remember thinking, "God have mercy on her soul." That was probably my initiation and preparation for some of the callers that phone me now on live TV while an entire nation watches how I respond.

How do you respond to the unsavory? What type of impact do you have on people? What type of impression do you leave? Are you a sweet savor or have your circumstances caused you to become so bitter and ugly that you have become a foul odor that is a stench in the nostrils of God? Or do you spend time with Him, soaking in the fragrance of the Lord, so that you carry the aroma of His love?

Those that abide in Him are destined to receive *'the crown of glory that fadeth not away'*. Those that don't are doomed to hear the words, *'Depart from me, I never knew you'*.

Richard Wurmbrand, who is known around the world as 'the Living Martyr' tells this story about a group of Romanian prisoners who were imprisoned and tortured solely for their faith. They were lined up naked before a firing squad, their clothes at their feet, and told that if they merely renounced Christ they could pick up their clothes, leave and not be executed. Only one man grabbed his clothes and left his place. The moment he did, one of the guards immediately threw down his rifle, started tearing off his clothes and ran for that vacant spot.

The commanding officer screamed and ranted, threatening to shoot him, but the young guard shouted back, "When that man left his place, a crown of glory appeared, rays shining down over his vacant spot, radiating and glowing, and if he does not want it, I do!"

~ 37 ~
There Is Only One Solution For These Chaotic Times

If there is ever a time that we need a Kairos Word from God, it is now. With all that is happening in the Middle East we need to know God´s mind and His directive at ´such a time as this´ We need to see like never before into the spirit realm so that truly we carry God´s burden and solution for such chaotic times. Yet, I meet people day after day that are not even remotely aware that they can attain this realm. It breaks my heart. God yearns to interact with us mortals whom He made in His own image; yet He is ignored. What leaves me dumbfounded are those that go to church week after week yet are oblivious to the fact that He is there amongst them and wants to have a meaningful encounter. Their only dissimilarity is that they made a decision somewhere long ago that they were not atheists and they made a commitment to live the Christian lifestyle. They miss God. They don´t have a revelation of Him.

On the other side of the coin, while I was in South Carolina for three months I was invited to a local church that does connect. It was the most incredible service that I had ever been to in my entire life. The praise and worship was electrifying. The people were totally fixated on God and immersed in His presence. I was so aware of the Personhood of Jesus there in that sanctuary that I thought He was going to materialize right before my very eyes. I thought, "It doesn´t get better than this!" Yet, each time I came back, it did. It got better and better and better.

One Sunday I was singing and trying to praise God harder somehow. I wanted to worship stronger, worship deeper. I knew there was more. I longed for the intense intimacy that I knew was possible as I was ushered right into the very throne room of God. I remembered back to when I was preaching at a church in Sarasota and I arrived three hours before the service to pray and meet with God. I picked up two flags at the back of the church and waved them high as I marched up and down the aisles praying and singing and praising God. As the service started I sensed a physical mantle descend from heaven, fold over me and engulf me totally. In the midst of that service people spoke out and said that I was glowing and radiating from the presence of God that was all over me.

During this service in South Carolina, as I sat in the 3rd pew from the back in a church of about 500 people, I thought, "If I only had a flag...." I opened my eyes and immediately noticed a man in the very front row pick up a red flag and walk down the center aisle, his eyes fixed directly on me and hand me the flag saying, "This is for you!" It´s almost beyond comprehension. I wanted a flag and God sent me a flag! That man was so tuned into God that he not only heard God´s directive but acted upon it in the middle of a church service.

I waved that flag as high as I could for an entire hour. I cannot explain in words the dimension of fellowship with God that I reached that day. The pastor never got to preach that Sunday as the entire congregation exploded with the knowledge of the presence of our Almighty God.

My friend Marcie lives in that dimension. She loves to pray. She prays for hours at a time. She was praying and reflecting upon

Psalm 27 when she had an experience much like John on the Isle of Patmos. She saw the Temple of Solomon clearly in the spirit. God showed her things beyond description. He gave her a revelation of a depth of love that she cannot describe. God shared His heart with her because she sought His face and desired, as this psalm says, to dwell in God's presence each day of her life and to behold the beauty of the Lord. God honored that. God will honor your quest for Him and reveal Himself to you as you have never imagined.

"And ye shall seek me, and find me, when ye shall search for me with all your heart. And I will be found of you, saith the Lord." Jeremiah 29:13, 14

He also wants to reveal Himself to those in the Middle East. He has already shown us a glimpse of His heart in Psalm 122 where He says, "Pray for the Peace of Jerusalem, they shall prosper that love thee."

Pray for the salvation of Israel. Pray for the salvation of the Palestinian people. They need a revelation of Jesus, the Messiah, the Prince of Peace!

~ 38 ~

God Has Stopped Talking To Me
--- Now He's Actually Shouting!

People have said to me, "I don't believe God talks to anybody." Well I can't wait to hear what they will say now that I'm professing that He is shouting at me but I will present the following and let the facts speak for themselves.

I'm confident these events will clearly demonstrate to the agnostics that not only is there a God but that He is involved in every aspect of our daily lives and that He encourages us and guides us through every aspect of our journey here on earth. I hope that not even an atheist will be able to miss hearing the undeniable voice of God and will not be able to pass it off as merely coincidence.

Since January, I have felt as if I'm swimming up stream. Obstacle after obstacle has been thrown in my path to hinder my race towards the things God has called me to do. The final straw that almost broke this camel's back occurred on a Friday. I did what any self-respecting, mature evangelist (that has faith to move mountains) would do -- I cried like a baby. I mean I really lost it! I sobbed. I couldn't hold it back. Anyone who knows me well knows that I never cry, so this was serious.

The following Monday my friend Sandy called to say the Lord had given her scripture for me the day before. It was II Corinthians chapter four. Although I was to read the entire chapter, I was to pay special attention to verse 16 which says, "Do not lose heart" because God was clearly saying, "Do NOT lose heart. Do NOT lose hope. Do NOT give up." It brought me a bit of comfort to know that the Lord was aware of my predicament. Moments after our conversation I reached for the book I had been reading and came across that very same scripture verse on the next page. This was definitely divine intervention so I called Sandy back to confirm that she had indeed heard from God.

The very next morning I went to read the daily devotional I receive from a prophetic ministry that I monitor. To my astonishment it was II Cor. 4:16. God was showing me how much He cared. Tears rolled down my face. I couldn't hold them back.

That finally did it. I got my focus realigned. All that mattered was that Jesus was coming back and in the meantime souls were perishing, so what was I going to do about it? Was I going to cry in my soup or continue to do everything I can to tell people that there is a God and that He loves them and wants to save them.

Obviously God thought I needed more convincing. On Thursday I decided to view the e-mail card that my friend Diane had sent me a few days earlier. It was of an eagle soaring high above the mountain tops. Underneath she added, "Donna, here's another scripture for you, II Cor. 4:8 and 9."

It was more than unbelievable. Beyond incredible. This was the fourth time in as many days that God was saying, 'Don't give up!" I guess He thought I might have a hearing problem or that I could still buckle and succumb under the weight of my load.

That is still not the end of this story though. Just before the Sunday morning service I decided to reread that chapter for the umpteenth time. I particularly concentrated on verses eight and nine, "we are afflicted in every way, but not crushed, perplexed, but not despairing, persecuted, but not forsaken, struck down, but not destroyed." Then I looked up and saw those exact words reflected on the wall from the overhead projector as the entire congregation sang, "Trading My Sorrows.."

Can you hear God's voice in this? I certainly can!

Oh, there's more --- today, just as I was typing this article, I received a sermon from the Watchman website. Do I need to tell you what scripture it was?

~ 39 ~

Don't Cry Over Spilled Milk

--- God Has Something Better

Ever since I was just a little kid my typical disposition was to never really want or expect much of anything. This all stemmed from an experience I had when I was five years old. Since there were no toys back in Croatia after the second world war, you can imagine my excitement when we came to Canada and I was given my very first doll. Sheer glee.

Now can you image the devastation the very next week when my parents decided to send it to some kid overseas that remained underprivileged? It had a profound effect on me and so altered my behavior that this is why I grew up to never desire anything because of this deep rooted fear of the heart-wrenching pain I would experience when it is yanked away from me. Although generally, when I wanted something, I just went out and worked harder or longer and purchased it but I held it loosely, just in case.

Since my husband and I worked very hard for 25 long years, we managed to attain quite a bit of wealth and possessions and had accumulated lands and houses. But like Job, 'the thing I feared the most' actually came upon us when we were embezzled back in 1991. Imagine the devastation. Almost immediately I reverted right back to my former mindset of desiring NO THING and was quite satisfied to espouse with the Apostle Paul that I was content whether I was abased or abounding. I certainly had no intention of striving for the next 25 years to amass it all back.

Instead, I figured out just how much I could live without and focused my priorities on the eternal instead. A very noble and idealistic concept until I discovered I didn't have the $1.99 needed to buy pantyhose. I got quite perturbed when I found my new budget did not allow for such luxuries. You can't go anywhere in Canada without pantyhose. You might get away with not wearing pantyhose in Florida, but not in Canada. People suspect something is amiss when your legs are bare in the middle of a blizzard. So naturally I explained to God that pantyhose were a necessity. Realizing God sometimes works in 'mischievous ways' I suspected that He's the one that arranged for my friend Marcie to get a secretarial job at a hosiery factory. She sent me a lifetime supply of hose in every shade under the sun. Imagine my excitement.

This is exactly how God responded to each and every need that arose in my life. He continued to provide over and above ---- until --- one incident this past summer. I have been relatively content, except for some minor grumbling and complaining, to live in a 30 foot trailer during the time we spend in Canada. Just when it felt as though it was getting smaller and smaller, I stumbled upon a little cottage nestled away in a Christian Campground. It was perfect right down to the oversized deck and huge maple tree in the front yard. Scoring 99 out of 100 points of the bells and whistles that I required and liked, it seemed to be a once in a lifetime find. Plus, a few of my friends already lived there. Imagine my excitement.

My dream was brutally shattered when I was denied approval to move into this campground because I held credentials outside of this denomination. Resubmitting applications, numerous appeals and torrents of tears fell on deaf ears. The Board would not reconsider. I began bombarding heaven and nagged God for six weeks to intervene and overrule their decision. In order to plead my case I invoked the scripture, *"Delight thyself also in the Lord; and He shall give you the desires of thine heart,"* but God chose not to comply.

Although I actually grieved the loss of that property, I realize that my Father in heaven knows what's best and He must have a different plan for this child. I trust His omniscience completely.

Now here comes my sermon, don't miss it: Denying or withholding what seems to be a blessing is not God's rejection of us or abasement against us. Instead it is a reflection of His love because it is a demonstration of His divine wisdom and foresight resulting in our ultimate good and well- being every single time. Therefore we need to stay excited about the things of God.

I would be in a sorry state if my happiness depended on material things, yet I believe He has a perfect little nest somewhere out there with my name on it. I intend to just delight in Him and wait for Him to surprise me. He loves to do that you know --- surprise His kids and bless their hearts. Just wait and see!

~ 40 ~
Heavenly Peace

A city full of people

All running to and fro

So much hurrying and scurrying

They are constantly on the go

They put up lights and decorate

Their houses in and out

But what I want to know my friend

Is, what's it all about?

After driving to the shops and malls

Buying gifts of every size

It's somewhere on the trip back home

That they come to realize

That they have spent more than they should

On all those toys and things

Yet off they'll go to get some more

Seeking the pleasure they think it brings

They wrap each box with ribbon and bow

And place it under the tree

Hoping it is just the thing

That will make Johnny squeal with glee

Yet, I know something is missing

And there is something very wrong

They are humming the familiar tune

But forgot the words to this most holy song

It's all about one special night

Two thousand years ago

The shepherds heard the wondrous news

When angels let them know

That in the town of Bethlehem

On this very sacred day

There beneath a shining star

The Lord of Glory lay

A multitude of heavenly host

Announced the glorious birth

Of this tiny babe who was and is

The Lord of heaven and earth

He came to show each one of us

God's everlasting love.

He's the image of His Father

Sent to us from heaven above

He is the Savior of the world

And came to set us free

He broke the chains of sin and death

For all eternity

Now we can sleep in total peace

For His Agape love surrounds us

So let us celebrate this time of year

By focusing on the Lord, Christ Jesus.

(Inspired by this picture of my grandson, Caleb laying in my son Steve's hand)

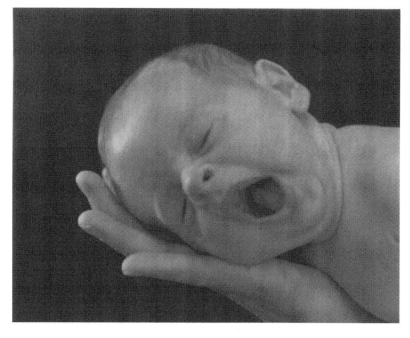

~ 41 ~

God Cleaned Up My Attitude With a Bar of Soap

As Christians we know exactly how to respond to the injustice in the world -- that's easy. We know we're to fall on our knees and bury our heads in prayer when wronged --- that's easier. We do not retaliate when we have been harmed and hurt --- hopefully. We believe in turning the other cheek --- usually. And, when someone asks us for our coat we graciously offer them our shirt as well.

Well, some of us do anyway. Realizing that reaching four out of five goals will in no way earn me a reprieve with God or anyone else either, I hope to at least clear my conscience y confessing and exposing this one little area in my life that sometimes gets the best of me. I don't mind giving. I always have been a giver. I love to give, but when anything is taken away from me I turn bright red, clench my fists, grit my teeth and flare my nostrils while thoughts of carnage race through my mind.

To make matters worse I justify my ungodly reaction as righteous indignation while screaming, "How dare they!" Actually 'screaming' is not the correct adjective, ranting and raving and carrying on would be a more accurate description of what happens as I clearly demonstrated just last week when a thief absconded with a valuable possession.

You might be thinking that since I was robbed that there is probably some justification to my behavior and you are more than willing to find it in your heart to forgive me. Well, read on because I am about to demonstrate why I should be flogged.

My husband and I drove to our clubhouse with the intention of spending a few minutes in the whirlpool. Naturally we would shower there rather than dry ourselves and put on all our clothes to go home and get undressed again redundantly repeating the entire process, so I brought along one of those little bars of soap that you get at any hotel in any city in North America.

I place it on the soap dish in the shower unit and stepped into the steaming tub. The one other person that was already in the water climbed out and entered the shower stall. She left a few moments later. I believe that you've already figured out the rest of this scenario, but I know you cannot even begin to envision what follows.

Picture an enraged, manic, soaking wet Christian running down the street in her bathing suit trying to overtake this little elderly lady yelling, "She took my soap! I can't believe anybody would steal a bar of soap" I was determined to catch her before she got too far and I told everyone along the way what had happened. Obviously, the explanations were necessary because I had to justify why I was running through a mobile home complex without a cover-up which is a major infraction.

I didn't know exactly what I was going to do or say when I caught her but it wad definitely not going to be pleasant for her. Fortunately, God caught up with me before I completely ruined my Christian witness that day over a 10-cent bar of soap.

I was reminded of the story in Matthew 18 where a king had forgiven a man an enormous debt and yet that same man went and hunted down someone who owed him just a little money and grabbed him by the throat and threw him in jail unmercifully.

I reflected on the enormity of sin God had forgiven me. For which Jesus Christ suffered a cruel and agonizing death on the cross and shed His blood so that I could be forgiven for my entire truckload of sin, yet I have the gall to be enraged over a bar of soap without displaying an ounce of mercy.

I went home and collected dozens of those little soaps and put them in a baggy and placed them in my car hoping to run into her again. I'm not too certain what I will say when I do but I know the Holy Spirit will give me the right words and help me display the love and forgiveness of Christ. It was only days later that my bill in a hardware store came to $13.76. I told the cashier that I would bring her the penny from the dashboard in my car. As she handed me back 24 cents she said, "That's what they all say. When you bring back the penny I will give you a quarter."

Instead of getting all bent out of shape and ranting and raving and carrying on, I went to my car and got all the nickels and dimes and quarters and pennies that were in the ashtray and I went back and said, "Here are some pennies for the next 159 people that come to your establishment."

My prayers are that God will help me obey Hebrews 12:14 which says, *"Follow peace with all men and holiness, without which no man shall see the Lord"* and Psalm 25:11, *"For thy name's sake, O Lord, pardon mine iniquity, for it is great."*

~ 42 ~

A Tribute to Christians, Past and Present

An interesting report on Christians called the Epistle to Diognetus was written in A.D.180 by an unknown author. He started out by saying, "Christians are not distinguished from the rest of mankind by country, by speech, nor by customs. They pass their days on Earth, but are citizens of heaven. They obey the established laws but at the same time surpass the laws by their lives." He lists some peculiarities of their lifestyles and then concludes by stating, "They love all and are persecuted by all. They are put to death and restored to life. They are poor yet make many rich. They lack all things yet abound in all things. They are abused and give blessing; they are insulted and repay the insult with honor. When they do good they are punished as evildoers; when they are punished they rejoice as those receiving life."

It was a very commendable testimony. What might the world say about Christians today? What makes them stand out? How are they different? What is their mode of operandi? What creed do they follow? I would not have known how to answer these questions 23 years ago. I grew up in a very dysfunctional family. Ever since I was 6 years old I could not depend on anyone. I was a latchkey kid and there was never anyone there for me so I learned to fend for myself from a very early age. Sometimes "fend" worked and sometimes it didn't, but I knew not to expect help from anyone, anytime, anywhere. Then one day, while raising a family of my own, I ran smack into the "family of God" and started relearning life's lessons as God demonstrated his unconditional, selfless love through these servants of Christ again and again.

The Apostle Paul said Jesus *"gave himself for us that he might redeem us from all iniquity and purify unto himself a peculiar people zealous of good works."* Especially on the Easter weekend I very much wanted you to be privy to how the family of God functions and at the same time I want to give thanks to God and a great big thanks to each one of them for all their zealous good works as they recently rallied around this very helpless, distraught couple.

Over a month ago, in the middle of the night, I summoned an ambulance for my husband who was in distress from congestive heart failure. He had an extremely severe heart attack complicated by water and blood in his lungs. He remained in critical condition, totally sedated and on life support for the next eight days, after which began another three weeks in Critical Care Units. During this difficult time we both received intensive care from another source, the "body of Christ." Some dear friends stood by me at 3 a.m. Many came and prayed at his bedside keeping an around-the-clock vigil. Our son, Dan, arrived immediately and stayed by my side, even when I slept at the hospital. We would go home just long enough to shower and change clothes and find food cooking in crock pots on the kitchen counter. Complete meals kept arriving the entire time. Phone calls, e-mail and cards arrived stating that an army of believers were praying for us. Some chauffeured me back and forth from the hospital. Others, knowing that we would eventually be air-lifted to Canada helped pack, close down our home and put lawn furniture away. Many held my hand, and all touched my heart.

The tiny air-ambulance allowed only one bag. I returned in the middle of winter with one change of clothes and no car. I could not even go home because it is not winterized. I was pleasantly surprised to find that God had an army waiting there, too. Even though they have nine children and one on the way, two of our precious friends opened up their home to me, gave me my own room and made me as welcome as a dearly beloved parent. They handed me the keys to one of their vehicles and said I could have it anytime to go anywhere for as long as I needed. They would not let me contribute for gas or groceries and literally gave us the shirts of their backs because we came with so few clothes. Then they paid the airfare for Dan to fly back to Jackson- ville after he delivered our car to Canada. Another couple drove our car up to Jacksonville to save him 10 hours of driving. Others sent prepaid calling cards. One sent pajamas and an extra suitcase. One sweet soul sent a money order that was far beyond generous. We were showered with love -- financially, physically, emotionally and spiritually.

The answers to the above questions are very clear to me. God's kids live out the words of the Apostle John from I John 3:16-18 *"By this we know love, because He (Jesus) laid down His life for us. And we also ought to lay down our lives for the brethren. But whoever has this world's goods, and sees his brother in need, and shuts up his heart from him how does the love of God abide in him? My little children, let us not love in word or in tongue, but in deed and in truth."*

They do. They demonstrate love, not just talk about it -- a very commendable testimony.

~ 43 ~

God's Guarantee Has a Never-Ending Warranty

Immediately after I became a Christian I became very convicted about smoking. I was determined to stop but it seemed to be a losing battle. The harder I tried to quit, the more I smoked. I spent more money trying to stop than on the habit itself. I would buy cigarettes by the carton to save money but then on my 'today-is-the-day-I'm-going-to-quit' rampages I'd break them all in half and throw them in the garbage. A few hours later I would dig them out and try lighting the short little butts without setting my nose of fire. When that didn't work my next plan of attack was to gather all my packs and throw them in the fireplace and watch them go up in smoke as I vowed NEVER to buy another package. During the night my nicotine level would drop dramatically so by the time the sun came up my entire body would be screaming for a nicotine fix. I would dig through the pile of ashes until I found a little piece that managed to survive the flames.

Learning from my past mistakes I then decided to bury my nasty habit by soaking the next carton in a sink full of water. You can not imagine how ludicrous and humiliated I felt digging through that soggy, disgusting mess the next morning trying to find something that could be lit to give me relief from the pain caused by this new experience of oxygen filling my lungs.

I was sincerely determined to succeed and thought that if I just got past the morning hump I could beat this thing. I realized I would have to find a more permanent way to dispose of these cancer sticks so I would buy a pack, smoke my 'this-is-going-to-be-my-last-puff' and throw the rest out my car window. One problem with that is that I became more convicted about littering than about smoking.

At this point I knew I needed divine intervention so I asked a lady who knew how to bombard heaven to pray for me. I didn't want her to know that I smoked so I merely said I had an unspoken request. A week later she told me that regardless of my request, God told her to simply pray peace for me.

PEACE? I thought peace was a dirty word. I had places to go, people to see and things to do. I was on roller skates for God. I didn't have time for peace. I presumed people that had peace sat still for hours at a time pondering and contemplating as they went nowhere and did nothing. I had the same misguided notions about peace that many people have about meekness.

Well, I noticed immediately that it did slow me down a little. Then a week later I felt like I was in slow motion. The week after, as if I was completely standing still. But when it seemed as if I started going backwards I started to yell, "Stop praying! STOP PRAYING! Don't pray peace for me any more! I can't get anything accomplished!" What I didn't realize was that I lived my life driven by the devil rather than being led by the Holy Spirit and although I thought I was accomplishing a lot of things, I was really sowing to the wind. They were totally unnecessary and had been causing me much anxiety. The anxiety was giving me an adrenaline rush which caused me to smoke even more to still my nerves, which caused me more anxiety. When I experienced the peace of God, peace replaced the anxiety, and I simply stopped smoking.

It was the peace that Isaiah 26:3 speaks about; *"Thou wilt keep him in perfect peace whose mind is stayed on thee, because he trusteth in thee. Trust ye in the Lord forever; for in the Lord Jehovah is everlasting strength."* Notice that the key is to focus on the Lord. Peace is guaranteed when we take our eyes off the circumstances and completely trust and rely on Him.

That supernatural peace was never more real to me than last week when I was rushing my husband to the hospital confident I'd get there before his heart attack became fatal. Prior to this night he had spent more than a month in intensive care because of congestive heart failure and had just recently been released. Now, just days later he started experiencing severe pain directly to his heart. As I raced to the hospital there was no fear. There was no panic. I had total peace as I quoted scripture after scripture the entire 45 minute drive knowing that God was in control and we were in the palm of His hand. Nothing could happen to either of us outside of His knowledge or permission.

Circumstances can not dictate our destiny. Our fate is totally and exclusively in the hands of God if we pray. Since He controls the winds and the waves we don't have to worry when storm clouds come our way. We don't have to lose our peace because, come what may, we have His never-ending unlimited warranty -- eternal life -- guaranteed and secured for all eternity!

~ 44 ~

God Certainly Has My Undivided Attention!

Just moments before I started this article I experienced goose bumps the size of ostrich eggs all over both my arms. I prefer to call them Holy Ghost bumps because the electrifying power and awesome presence of God permeated my entire being. I became unmistakably aware of His insistence regarding the topic of this article and His 'hand's on' involvement in it's message. I could hardly wait to get it on paper.

As I finished typing last month's article I was prompted to include a note to myself as a reminder of what I felt should be the scripture for this month. I normally never have even an inkling.

Over the course of this month three different people, who are each very close friends of mine, quoted the exact scripture during our separate conversations. Each time I chirped in excitedly "YES, that's EXACTLY what my next article is about!" I felt I was receiving distinct confirmation from God and my spirit stirred each time.

I know there are some reading this that doubt God's participation in this kind of every day, moment by moment involvement in anyone's life and you are not at all convinced that these could be divinely appointed, supernaturally inspired, God ordained conversations and statements. I hope you are sitting down because God is about to display His desire to have that kind of relationship with you as I relate the events that just took place.

My life had been on fast forward during the 74 days my husband spent in the hospital but seemed to accelerate once he was released. Being a caregiver to someone that has had open heart surgery is a little overwhelming therefore I couldn't find even a moment to start writing this article. Since my deadline was fast approaching it was necessary to begin this afternoon but I wanted to first check my e-mail to see if there was anything urgent that needed my attention. There were more than 35 that needed to be answered so I decided to forgo opening any of them and let them accumulate until I could give them the appropriate attention they deserved because this was much more pressing. Yet while browsing quickly over the subject lines I was compelled to open a particular one called 'Daddy's Prayer' and found that the scripture accompanying the story was the very verse I was about to type. This is when I became so elated that I almost cried because it became glaringly apparent that this message was foremost on God's heart and that He is placing special emphasis on this subject. I believe that each reader will know in their own heart what they need to do with the prompting in James 5:16 '......*the effectual fervent prayer of a righteous man availeth much*'.

Might I add that 'the prayers of many availeth even more'? During the past three month's that my husband was at death's door repeatedly, it became very obvious that it was because of the prayers of our family and friends that his life was spared so many times. Those fervent and unceasing prayers also seemed to place me inside an invisible cocoon made of love and faith in which I continuously experienced the peace and rest of God. I was not phased by my circumstances even once. Then one morning, right after I informed everyone that he was out of the hospital, I awakened to find my prayer cover had lifted. The difference was like night and day. I felt the strain of the past months closing in. My husband felt like he had been put through a meat grinder. Scurrying to the phone and to my computer I sent out an urgent SOS ..... "Please DON'T STOP PRAYING! I can tell you stopped! Please keep praying. It makes all the difference in the world!! "

New prayers must have gone up immediately because I felt as if I was bathed in warm honey once again. My husband commented that he could actually feel the prayers surrounding us like a thick, high wall.

This article was almost completed up to this point but I knew I needed at least another paragraph to connect my closing thoughts. Before putting on the final touches I decided I first needed to make a phone call. (discovered later it was actually God's prompting) Someone had called me days before and I completely forgot to return her call. As we were finishing our conversation she commented, "I just want to say this one final thing; I don't know where it is in the bible but a scripture is coming to my mind" She then tried to quote the following by memory, *'For the eyes of the Lord search back and forth across the whole earth, looking for people whose hearts are perfect toward Him* (pray to Him and seek Him) *so that He can show His great power in helping them'*.

Since my spirit leaped just as high as it did earlier I quickly looked it up and found it in II Chronicles 16:9. The incredibly amazing point that jumped out at me was that this scripture was cross-referenced to James 5:16 in my bible. I don't know about you, but God certainly has my attention! He wants us to PRAY!

Our petitions and requests to God are not only an extremely powerful resource but God is looking for a people who will pray to Him much more often about everyone and anyone and about everything and anything. God loves it when we talk to Him! It blesses God's heart and it also makes all the difference in the world.

~ 45 ~

Jesus Loved to Tell Stories

During His three year ministry on earth Jesus taught God's precepts and revealed life changing truths through parables. The entire bible is a compendium of thousands of stories about people very much like ourselves, with similar likes and dislikes, hopes and dreams, who had to deal with every day problems and hardships. Their stories clearly demonstrate that when they did things 'God's way' they had victory in every area of their lives.

As everyone knows, I love to tell stories about what God has done in my own life. As a matter of fact this is why I chose Psalm 40 to be the name of my ministry. It reads, *"He lifted me up also, out of the horrible pit, out of the miry clay and set my feet upon a rock and established my goings. He has put a new song in my mouth, even praise unto our God; others shall see what He has done for me and put their trust in Him"*.

People will 'see what He has done for me' and they will be able to relate to my situations and apply my principles to their own lives while they glean wisdom from my experiences and learn valuable lessons from my mistakes. Through my stories I hope to impart faith into hopeless situations so that people will be able to trust God implicitly and know that His ultimate goal is their eternal (and temporal) well-being.

Last fall I wrote about how I desperately needed to buy something much bigger than the trailer which we had been staying in during the months we spent in Canada and how my dream to buy a little cottage was unexpectedly shattered. God did not seem to want to intervene on my behalf. He just ignored me in spite of my begging and pleading and whining, yet I stated emphatically in that article that I completely trusted His divine wisdom and foresight even though I felt crushed and even though I thought it would have been the ideal solution considering how cramped our living arrangements had been over the past seven years. Anything else within a hundred miles was five times the price.

Months later, in the middle of March, as we were being air-ambulanced back to Canada because of my husband's health, I had to wonder why my plans to purchase that cottage were blocked. I arrived with one bag and open-toed sandals just as two separate blizzards hit Ontario. Living at our trailer was NOT an option. I knew God HAD to do something!

Not only did He DO something..... He had been making preparations for months. Our friends Penny and Anthony bought a huge home even though they really had no intention of relocating to another city at that time. The 100 year old house was just too good a deal to pass up, so they scooped it up and were convinced it was all according to God's miraculous plan and perfect timing because they now had more than enough room to take me in out of the cold. They gave me the key to their house and the keys to their van and said, "Welcome to our family. Make yourself at home. Come and go as you please, for as long as you need."

I marveled at God's provision but knew that since my husband would not be able to climb stairs when they released him from the hospital that he could not sleep on their living room sofa indefinitely. Our only solution was to move him to their cottage which just happened to be at the very same Christian Campground where the management had rejected us.

It was perfect. Not too big and not too small. And, whenever I walked through the fabulous compound and especially as I passed by the church I felt as though I was on holy ground. Day after day as my eyes feasted on the two hundred year old trees, the lilacs, the chipmunks, the birds and acres of cozy little cottages I thought my heart might break. I ached for such a place and thought heaven could not be much better than this!

I'm still not quite certain how it actually happened and the details are a bit of a blur, but by the middle of June our friends cottage became ours. Since they now lived only minutes away they realized it would be redundant to keep it. We applied to buy it and this time were instantly approved.

God somehow intervened and opened the door that had been slammed shut, on top of which, it was 30% cheaper than the one that I tried to buy last year. I'm not even going to try to figure it out, I'm just going to thank Him every day of my life and tell as many people as I can about this most incredible God that I serve.

~ 46 ~

A Miracle is About to Happen

When a friend of mine who is an evangelist came to town, I asked my friend Dave to come to her church service and to expect a miracle because his kidneys had shut down and he was on dialysis. He was also a brand-new Christian and very skeptical that God would or could do anything. After some arm twisting, he reluctantly agreed. When Rev. Ursula said, "There is someone here who has kidney disease -- please stand up because God is going to heal you," Dave stood up but instead of waiting for her to pray, or acknowledging that he had the disease, he walked out of the building and never came back.

Since I was more than eager to find out why he left, I called him after the service even though it was very late. He admitted that he thought it was a hoax. It was just impossible for him to believe that an evangelist could call him out like that. He was certain that I had talked to her about his condition.

After I convinced him that I had not even mentioned him or his disease to her but that she was operating in the "gift of a Word of Knowledge" as recorded in I Corinthians 12:8, he agreed to come to my home the next night for prayer.

I assured him that God would not reveal or call out his disease unless he intended to heal him and then my husband and I prayed for him to be healed, believing that as long as we have a relationship with Jesus Christ, we can expect no limitations.

The famous evangelist Kathryn Kuhlman said, "It is when active faith dares to believe God to the point of action that something has to happen."

The next time I heard from Dave was from his hospital bed. He related how the very next morning after we had prayed for him his doctor had called and said they had a donor organ and that it was a perfect match, which was a miracle in itself because for every kidney that becomes available, there are thousands waiting in line. The second miracle was that his body was not rejecting the transplant.

I was glad to see that he realized it was an act of God since his chances of having a transplant were almost zero. He knew it was an answer to our prayers and Rev. Ursula's "Word of Knowledge" and he gave God all the glory.

Sometimes God does an instantaneous miracle and a person is immediately healed. Other times when God heals it takes a segment of time for the body to go through the process of restoration and rejuvenation. Still at other times, as in the case of Dave, he uses doctors and medicine. But even then, doctors can cut and sew and stitch but they do not have the power or ability to heal. That comes from God alone.

Having said all that, I want to share something incredible that happened just last week. My husband and I were at church listening to a visiting evangelist when he pointed me out and asked if I had a son. When I answered that I had three, he said that God was about to do something wonderful in my family. Something awesome.

When I told him that I had a son who has multiple sclerosis, the evangelist said that the Spirit of the Lord told him that he wanted to do something for our son. Then he prayed for our son Michael and said a mighty miracle would take place supernaturally in him as my husband and I lay hands on him and pray for him. He decreed that Michael will be a recipient of the power and the fire of almighty God and that he would be healed.

Although we have not seen evidence of that 'Word of Knowledge' yet, we are believing that the healing has already happened in the spirit realm, the moment God called it out through the evangelist and that is just a matter of time before its manifested in the physical realm.

Naturally, my prayer is that God would give understanding and wisdom to the researchers so that they would find a cure for MS and that thousands of others would benefit also. So please join with me in prayer for all those who are disabled because of this terrible condition.

~ 47 ~

Santa's Gift to Jesus

Did you hear about what Santa Claus gave Jesus for Christmas? The ONE thing that Jesus didn't have. The ONLY thing that Jesus would literally die for. The ONE thing that He craved unashamedly and heaven awaited expectantly. The ONE thing He is going to treasure for all eternity. The ONE thing that caused all the angels of God to dance a jig like it was the 4th of July.

If you don't know the answer by now -- you definitely need to keep reading because Santa Claus figured it out last summer.

Actually he was not the REAL Santa Claus but that's what my husband named Jerry, his Saturday morning garage sale buddy because he so resembled the beloved character. He had all the little kids fooled too. They would ask what he was bringing them for Christmas and he would laugh and say, "I'm going from yard sale to yard sale, looking for it now."

His suspenders created an unintentional added dimension to the Santa image because they were the only way he could hold his pants up over his ever expanding physique. And I am certain he grew that long white beard just to hide the many stains on his tee-shirt. Doing laundry was not his top priority. He would wear something for weeks and then throw it out and get something fresh at the next tag sale. You could easily describe him as slovenly. Just one look and you could tell he needed a wife. My husband would be just as bad, if not worse, if I ever took a sabbatical and Venice would then end up with two sloppy, messy Santa impersonators driving around every Saturday morning.

I describe how unkempt he was so that you can grasp how very special this story really is

This past summer while we were in Canada we got a call from his daughter saying that Jerry was on his deathbed and that she and the family had come down from Ohio. He could hardly breathe but he kept saying he had to wish Darko a Merry Christmas. It took them a week but they finally figured out who Darko was and where we were. At that point they did not expect him to last through the night.

Even though he was gasping and struggling for every breath, I lead him through a prayer over the phone which ensured where he would spend eternity. He asked God to forgive him his sins and he accepted Christ as his Lord and Savior for the very first time. Then he went into coma.

Almost a week later, his daughter called again and said he passed away but couldn't wait to tell me what happened though. Just before he died, Jerry came to and said, "I want my shoes and a nice shirt and pants too. I want to look nice because I'm going to meet Jesus!" They argued that he couldn't have his trousers because of all the tubes and the catheter and everything else attached to him but he kept insisting and kept repeating the phrase over and over until finally they cut out a large hole in his pants to accommodate all the tubes. Then, with a smile on his face, Jerry closed his eyes and stepped into eternity.

Jerry gave Jesus the one thing He didn't have --- himself. Since it is His birthday, why don't you consider doing the same. Give

Him your heart. You don't even need to clean yourself up, just come as you are. He awaits with arms wide open.

~ 48 ~

She Has the Problem ...But God Fixes Me

Have you ever been suddenly dropped like a hot potato by a friend whom you have loved unconditionally? Was it especially painful to you because you bent over backwards to accommodate their every need and consistently helped to solve just about every problem in their life? Did it come as a tremendous shock to you because you endeavored to make yourself available at every opportunity and whenever possible? Was it a friend who called every time that they needed encouragement or a shoulder to cry on and you willingly and naturally complied? Did you do just about everything for them including jumping through a few hoops?

Well then, take heart, you are not alone. It has happened to me too. To make matters worse, I'm the person who persuaded this gal to become a Christian. I was her spiritual Mom. She sat just two rows in front of me in church. Suddenly one day she began going to great lengths to avoid me. Even when the pastor would say on Sunday mornings, "Turn around and great one another with the love of the Lord", she would shake hands with everyone within five pews but skip over me as if I were invisible. She would totally avoid eye contact and turn her head with an overly animated, exaggerated motion. This went on for months until one day I couldn't stand it any longer and I took my purse and whopped her with it, (yes, its true, I actually did that) quizzically asking, "Good morning??? Hello???" Weeks later I smacked her with my two pound bible (you might be shocked but she wasn't) thinking I'd surely get some sort of reaction out of her that time. She never even flinched.

At that time I was not a person that would confront a situation head on so my solution was to just let sleeping dogs lie but God had a totally different plan. He decided that I should get a card and write her a note asking her to forgive me. I couldn't believe it. Forgive me for what? "Whatever she has perceived that you had done", was His response.

It was the hardest thing that I ever did. It totally went against every fiber in my being. I hated to submit and to bend to an arrogant, haughty spirit but I knew that I had to obey God.

You just can't imagine how overjoyed I was when I got to church the next Sunday and realized she was not even there. I was elated. I was certain that God would not expect me to actually grovel in this manner but that He merely wanted to see if I would obey Him.

You certainly wouldn't have a far reach to imagine how I felt that evening when the Lord asked me to read my note to her in front of the entire congregation. I argued, "Lord what will people think that I did to her? - Lord, why would you humiliate me in this way? - How can you do this to me?"

It was no use. I knew, that I knew, that He would not let me off the hook, even though I did not understand why. I came to the front of the church, my face beat red, my eyes fixed on the floor and mumbled, "Dear Friend; please forgive me for whatever I did to offend you. Whatever it was I am sorry, it was not intentional. I would be very willing to discuss it with you, but if you don't wish to talk about it, I understand. Your friend in Christ, Donna."

The church was silent for probably an entire five minutes. There was a holy hush. Then one by one people started to get up out of their seats and go over and hug and love on one another. You could hear their muffled sobs. Tears flowed unashamedly. God was healing hurts and reconciling hearts. It continued for three consecutive Sundays.

It amazes me how we can ignore scriptures like Matthew 5:23 & 24 (NKJV) which say, *'Therefore if you bring your gift to the altar, and there remember that your brother has something against you, leave your gift there before the altar, and go your way. First, be reconciled to your brother, and then come and offer your gift.'* and 1 John 4:20 which says *'If someone says, "I love God," and hates his brother, he is a liar; for he who does not love his brother whom he has seen, how can he love God whom he has not seen?'*

So our obligation is to reconcile our broken relationships privately before God needs to humble us by asking us to do it publicly. It doesn't matter who's right or who's wrong, we just need to go and fix it.

However Painful, Upon Request, Relinquish To It's Rightful Owner

Since my entire weekend was going to be preoccupied with overnight guests and family, whom I had not seen since last fall, my concern was that I would not have an opportunity to write an article (this article) in time for my Monday morning deadline. I would not have been as anxious had I at least one single thought in my head. My mind was totally blank even though I had been praying intermittently for days asking God for an idea, a scripture or ANYTHING which would give me even the slightest indication of what was on His heart for this month.

God was silent. There was not even an inkling of a message, much less one in it's entirety, but I was confident that God would not leave me in the lurch so I determined to not let this hinder my spending quality time with my boys and my company.

After supper we were all sitting around sharing stories about the things that greatly impacted and influenced our lives. I happened to remember a very powerful and dramatic story that I had read years ago from Richard Wurmbrand's devotional that became a tremendous lesson by which I have since governed my own life. As I was relating the story, my husband's shoulders started shaking and he began to sob. Our friend Anthony also started to weep and wipe tears from his eyes. I looked around the room and realized how much it had touched everyone's heart and then I thought, "I HAVE an article for Monday."

It is powerful. It is moving. It will melt your heart. It could have such an impact on you that for the rest of your life it may change your response to those things that go drastically and unexpectedly wrong or your response when situations arise that are beyond your control.

The story was about a pastor and his wife who had two little boys. One day while the pastor was at work the boys climbed up the tree which was in their yard as they had done many times before. Unfortunately on this sad day they climbed just a little higher and the branch they were on broke and they fell to their deaths.

Upon finding both her sons lying dead on the ground, the mother gently picked up one boy and carried him upstairs and laid him on his bed and then did the same with the other son. When her husband arrived home and enquired about the boys she simply stated that they were upstairs and that they would be having dinner without them because she wanted to discuss a serious problem with him.

She then proceeded to tell her husband that even though she was not a very vain woman that she had borrowed a set of diamond earrings from her neighbor. She went on to explain that while he was at work she would put them on and gaze in the mirror and admire how beautiful they looked on her. She explained how they glistened and sparkled and how wonderful they made her feel. She was relating how much joy they brought her when her husband interrupted, "There is nothing wrong with that. You're just a typical woman. Why would that be a problem?"

She answered, "Well the problem is, today our neighbor asked to have them back." To which her husband immediately replied, "You HAVE to give them back. They're not yours to keep."

At this point she took his hand and led him upstairs to where their sons were laid out on their beds and said, "Years ago God sent us these two precious jewels but today He asked to have them back."

As tears flowed, her distraught husband then remarked, "I'm so thankful that God has given me a wife who is so wise and who trusts so implicitly in His sovereignty."

~ 50 ~

So, How Was YOUR Week?

Close your eyes and picture yourself sitting in a tiny little cottage nestled in the midst of a very picturesque landscape surrounded by 100 year old, 80 foot tall Canadian maple trees. Each tree is covered with these huge, overloaded limbs, stretching majestically across the open sky. That part is easy to imagine. But now, picture these trees crashing and falling down all around you like pins at the bowling alley.

It was SCARY!

Normally I love a good, old-fashioned thunderstorm but I never bargained for anything like this. After all, this is Ontario and I've not seen a serious storm in my entire life up here. Now I'm watching lightening bolt after lightening bolt cracking and hitting the ground on every side around us. I must have jumped three feet in the air at one loud flash right outside my living room window. Cars were leaving the campground one after another. Right after my hubby just about peeled me off the ceiling, I turned to him and said in a very high-pitched, stress-laden voice, "OK, maybe we SHOULD leave!" Then I thought, 'No, if God has decided that my number's up today, one of these trees would simply fall and crush me right there in my car as we were leaving the property. God would find me even if I was hiding under my bed!' Then, on a more spiritual note, as I came to realize that at any moment I could simply end up in the arms of Jesus, beholding the face of God, all apprehension left. The peace of God flooded my body, soul and spirit and I was very aware that my destiny was in the hands of my Creator. Still, I did negotiate with Him that if I had my 'druthers', I'd 'druther' live to see another day!.

Another lightening bolt struck within feet of my window and the heavy thud that followed caused me to think that one of those trees actually struck our cottage. I looked through our front door and could hardly believe the sight. This very dense, yet pure white, water was swirling sideways, in an upward motion. A fierce wind was propelling it at a record breaking speed. I tried to reason that rain falls DOWN and falls OUT of the sky. It doesn't try to go back up. I couldn't even see our fire-engine red van, which was parked only five feet from my door, through the thick, white, wall of water.

The tornado was over in a matter of minutes. Along with many other stunned and shaken cottage owners, we ventured out to access the damage and found an aftermath of carnage. The cottage almost directly behind us had a tree toppled on top of it. It was the loud thud that I had felt earlier. The amazing thing was that it looked like someone had gently placed it on top of their roof because there was no damage to the structure, even though the tree's trunk was probably about eight feet around.

Another cottage was suspended in midair. The root system had lifted it high up off the ground. It was laying across the power lines so it didn't come crashing down on top of the cottages across the road. One of the tallest and thickest trees, which was directly in front of my friend's place, was uprooted and lay pointing away from her cottage, totally in the opposite direction. Another huge tree fell very conveniently BETWEEN two trailers doing only minimal damage, destroying just their awnings and decks.

After accessing the entire situation, it was more than obvious that the hand of God intervened on our behalf cradling us as a hen does her chicks, deliberately orchestrating the sovereign outcome. Not a single person was hurt. Not a hair on anyone's head was harmed. It reminded me of the airplane crash that happened just days prior to this. An Air-France jet crashed at the Toronto airport and all 309 people escaped unharmed even though it burst into flames and then burned to the ground within minutes. It also immediately reminded me of Psalm 91 which I encourage you to tuck away for a time when you might be in need of divine intervention. *"He that dwelleth in the secret place of the most High shall abide under the shadow of the Almighty. I will say of the Lord, He is my refuge and my fortress: my God; in Him will I trust. Surely He shall deliver thee from the snare of the fowler, and from the noisome pestilence. He shall cover thee with His feathers and under His wings shalt thou trust; His truth shall be thy shield and buckler. Thou shalt not be afraid for the terror by night; nor for the arrow that flieth by day; Nor for the pestilence that walketh in darkness, nor the destruction that wasteth at noonday. A thousand shall fall at thy side; and ten thousand at thy right hand; but it shall not come nigh thee.... Because thou hast made the Lord, which is my refuge even the most High, thy habitation; There shall no evil befall thee, neither shall any plague come nigh thy dwelling. For He shall give His angels charge over thee, to keep thee in all thy ways. They shall bear thee up in their hands, lest thou dash thy foot against a stone.* (KJV)

~ 51 ~
Don't Just Pretend To Be My Friend

If there is one thing that I am thankful for in my life it is that God has put friends in my life that love me enough to tell me the truth. No matter how painful. No matter how much it might hurt. The unadulterated plain and simple corrective criticism that we all need from time to time that causes us to become better people. And, I especially appreciate it since I realize that they are taking the chance that I might not want to hear the truth, get my back up and sever our relationship even though they are doing it for my own good. I see them as being 'true friends' in the deepest sense of the word because their ultimate goal is to see me become the kind of person that God wants me to be.

One such friend is Bette. One day she started acting a bit cool and reserved, as if she was merely a polite guest visiting me, rather than a buddy. I sensed the strain in our relationship almost immediately. I cautiously watched from a distance for a while and then I outright confronted her expecting that I had committed some serious breach against her. After being pressured a little she finally blurted, "You parked in a wheelchair parking spot!"

I started processing what she had just said. I thought she was joking. There was total silence for what seemed like five minutes until I realized she was not going to say anything else. No, there was nothing else. She was serious. That was it. That was what was causing the tension even though I knew that she knew that I was in very excruciating pain because of my back on the day in question. She also knew that I had a wheelchair parking permit hanging in my van.

The first thing that reared it's ugly little head in my spirit was, "Oh boy, if THAT'S ALL you've got on me, I'm more wonderful than I thought. Ho ho ho, I must be pretty special if that's all you can come up with against me."

Even after discussing the situation with her at great length and trying to convince her that I was justified for using my husband's permit, she would not relent and said it compromised my integrity. Now that's what I call a pretty serious accusation! I argued that it would be absolutely assinign for me to first go to a doctor's office to prove my back hurts, then send away to Canada for a sticker that takes six weeks to process. By then I would not need my own sticker.

Fortunately, I had enough wisdom to tell her that I was going to take it up with the Lord. But before talking to God about the situation I told my husband why Bette had acted like she had an axe to grind. He couldn't stop laughing because the one thing I constantly and relentlessly harp at him about is not parking in those spaces on the days that he feels well and is able to walk further and I insist he leave those spots instead for someone who can't. (Since he critiques these articles that I write, maybe he'll get convicted and stop -- heeheehee, we'll see)

When I finally asked God for His perspective on this situation the response caused me to want to crawl under a rock. Since my husband's permit had his name on the back and not mine, that meant that a police officer would have every legal right under the law to issue me a ticket. Since I could be fined $200.00, that meant that I MUST BE breaking a law.

The revelation absolutely stunned me. Me? Donna? Breaking the law? Even as a kid I was a stickler for rules and regulations and obeying my parents! People have always said that my honesty borders on stupidity and yet here I was, totally blind and oblivious to something that was not only against the law, but could cause strangers, or maybe even someone that would recognize me from my picture in this paper, or someone that had come to one of my speaking engagements to think of me in a much different light than I should be projecting.

None of us are where God needs us to be. We have blind spots. We have weaknesses. We also have very conditioned behavioral patterns that we do not realize might be offensive to others, not to mention offensive to God. Therefore, since *'iron sharpens iron'* (Proverbs 27:17 KJV) we indisputably need each other. We need each other's expertise. We need each other's wealth of knowledge and insight.

So since God, in His wisdom, uses each and every believer in Christ as an instrument and tool to help form the nature and character of Christ in us, I pray He fills your life with friends such as this and I pray that this Thanksgiving you have an opportunity to celebrate that friendship together.

~ 52 ~

One God, One Mind, One Message

There is something very interesting that occurred about twenty minutes after I submitted last September's article for my Monday morning deadline. Actually, it's quite miraculous! I went to check my e-mail and came across one from a close friend that was marked, 'A MUST READ!'. Naturally, I opened it first. It contained a very lengthy article, written by a very well-known author who has published more than 20 books. Amazingly, his message was almost identical to the article that I had just written and sent off to the Gondolier and the similarities were so numerous that they were almost word for word, even down to such unique words and adjectives like 'unimaginable'.

Whenever something like this happens it is such a tremendous confirmation to me because it shows me that I am truly hearing from God. It confirms that I am clearly hearing what He is saying to me because He is telling so many of His other messengers the same thing, at the same time. As 2 Peter 1:21 declares; *"It is the Holy Spirit within us that enables us to speak the messages of God".* A similar reference is made in Ephesians 3:5 which says that God clearly reveals His divine truths to us through the power of the Holy Spirit.

My first such experience happened about 10 years ago. After I composed a sermon which I was preparing for a church in South Carolina, I dictated it onto a cassette tape. I finished the message just as two friends arrived to take me to a meeting up in Sarasota where John Bevere, another well-known author and minister, was speaking. At the time though I had never even heard of John

Bevere. Since the drive to Sarasota was going to take about forty minutes, the exact length of my message, my friends agreed to listen to it on the way there.

After the service, while perusing the book table, I felt the Lord strongly impressing me to get a book called, 'The Devil's Door'. Well, that posed a problem because I was in no financial position to spend $10 on a book. Secondly, I had brought absolutely no money with me, so why was the Lord insisting that I needed to read that book? Finally, in desperation, I said, "Lord, if you want me to read that book, then you'll just have to have it pop up at the next garage sale that I visit because I have no intention of borrowing the money from my friends. There are much more pressing issues to spend $10 on!"

Turning away from the book table I saw my friends, now standing with John Bevere, motioning for me to come and join them. As I approached, they were telling him that I was about to leave to minister in South Carolina. To my amazement, he spun around and very adamantly stated, "Go and get my book, The Devil's Door. Read it and go preach it. If you cannot afford to buy it, just take it. Please, go spread the message."

I must have looked like a deer in headlights as the realization hit me that this was a divinely orchestrated encounter. I grabbed the book and could hardly wait to get home and find out what God so very adamantly wanted me to read and know. You cannot imagine the shear panic that gripped me when I discovered that John Bevere's book was not only on the same Old Testament chapter and verse that my message was on, but he even used the same New Testament scriptures to back up his message. Additionally, he had a very similar personal experience happen to him as did to me, except his occurred at a baseball game while mine was an incident that happened on the front steps of a friend's house, but the gist of both our situations was absolutely identical.

My immediate reaction was that people would think that I had first read his book and then plagiarized most of it. My mind raced because I didn't know what to do. I almost picked up the phone to call my friends who could prove that I did not, since they had listened to my tape and knew that I had never even heard of this man until that night.

Suddenly, God's peace descended like manna from heaven and I received a very simple, yet astonishing revelation. It is a revelation that continues to be a source of encouragement each and every time I prepare a new message, allowing me to be totally confident that the things which I write and preach are not just my own words and ideas but they come form the very heart of God, revealed to me by the Spirit of God. It is straight from I Corinthians 2: 12-16 ; *"Now we have received, not the spirit of the world, but the spirit who is from God, that we might know the things that have been freely given to us by God. These things also we speak, not in the words which man's wisdom teaches, but which the Holy Ghost teaches; comparing spiritual things with spiritual ... we have the mind of Christ."* (NKJV)

~ 53 ~

"....Ye have not, because ye ask not"

You would think that after having spent more than 25 years serving God and reading in His word what we are supposed to do, that some things would come just naturally and automatically to me. Not always. I hang my head in shame and admit to you, in print yet, that sometimes I never even THINK to pray.

Oh, don't get me wrong, I pray all the time, every day, about everything, but I'm talking about those times when some unexpected crisis catches me by surprise and instead of taking it to God immediately, I end up running around like a chicken with my head cut off. One such recent example, which I believe you will enjoy hearing about, happened last month, just three days before I was to appear on the live call-in television program which I host periodically. We were having Sunday dinner with friends when I realized to my horror that the very hard and sharp object in my mouth was nothing that the chef had prepared. Upon close examination I discovered it was the entire top of a tooth from a very visible location in my mouth. My only consolation was that I hadn't swallow it and also that attached to this tooth was a metal post, indicating that root canal had been performed at some point, so I was pretty confident that I was not going to have any pain.

At least not any actual physical pain. Although seeing myself with a gap near the front of my mouth, where a tooth needed to be, just days before appearing before the entire nation, certainly caused me some very strong psychological trauma. So naturally,

I considered this a most earth-shattering catastrophe that needed to be rectified immediately. Unfortunately, all the dental clinics and dentists that I contacted did not seem to share the same opinion. I couldn't get an appointment for weeks even though I explained that the sharp stub in my mouth was cutting my tongue and I feared I could end up with blood trickling from my mouth, on camera, live, for the whole world to see, because I would be talking nonstop for three solid hours.

Finally, I reluctantly resolved to call a dentist who had wanted more than $35,000 to fix my husband's teeth about 10 years ago, because he at least had our name of file. Since we could buy two automobiles for that kind of money we never went near him again but at this moment in time I threw caution to the wind and called there. The earliest appointment they could give me was for the Monday AFTER the television program, which was not going to help my vanity but I realized this situation could develop into an infection, so I agreed. Then, realizing I had just booked an appointment with the most expensive dentist on the entire west coast of Florida, it finally dawned on me to pray and ask God to rebuke the devourer (Malachi 3:11) from needlessly robbing me of my financial resources. Especially of not robbing me the month before I needed extra cash to travel to Canada. Plus, my son was about to get married AND we were expecting a new grandbaby. Every single dollar was categorically assigned.

To make a very long story short, God's supernatural provision started to unfold as I looked out the window and noticed my neighbor's furniture strewn all over her front lawn. Curiosity getting the best of me, I sauntered over there and found a couple of people, whom I knew, installing carpet in her lanai. While chit chatting with them I mentioned how I had unsuccessfully spent the entire morning trying to find a dentist who could help me right away, to which they replied, "We have an excellent dentist who is right around the corner. Call him!" Only trouble was, neither of them could remember his name.

This was a completely God-ordained memory lapse because it compelled me to drive there, tooth in hand, instead of just picking up the phone and calling, because I would have been told that the dentist was not in, but at home with a bad back. Therefore, as I was explaining my predicament to the receptionist, his assistant came out and said she could see me right then and there and try to do something for me.

For the next 20 minutes she took X-rays; cleaned the shaft; tried to position the tooth back in place; filed it down a bit; had me grind down on the purple paper; tried fitting it again; filed it down a little more; used more purple paper; did more grinding; fitted it again; filed it some more until it fit; then dried the shaft; and finally cemented the tooth in place. As she handed me the tube of cement to take home with me for future use, she said, "Since I don't know if this job is going to last one day, one month or forever, I'm not even going to charge you!"

Oh, to think how many times I needlessly feared and fretted that I would not have enough money for something, instead of simply praying and trusting God who is more than able to meet every need. Shame on me.

~ 54 ~

Why Don't I Do This More Often?

My good friend Penny made a profound statement yesterday. She said, "Every morning as I'm getting up I say, 'Lord, I want to bless you today. What can I do to bless YOU?'." What an absolutely novel concept! How very refreshing too in a day when everyone seems to have joined a 'Bless ME, God' club and have developed a self-centered 'this is what I want FROM YOU, God' mentality.

Just imagine a world where people are focused on being a blessing rather than looking to BE blessed. I'm certain God would be thrilled. Probably very shocked too.

I remember one particular day when I did do that. It looked like I was actually going to have a day off. I didn't have any phone calls to make or e-mail to answer. No articles to write or sermons to prepare. My house was dusted. My garden was weeded. All our clothes were laundered. My bills were paid and filed away and even my windows were washed. For once it seemed my life was completely on track but that posed a very unique problem because I was not accustomed to taking a day off. I didn't know how to act. I didn't know what to do next. I wondered if I should even bother to get dressed or brush my teeth or should I just continue to sit in my kitchen sipping my coffee staring off into space? Finally I said, "Please God, don't let me just waste this day. Let me be a blessing to someone today."

It amazes me how lickety split God answered that prayer because it wasn't even ten o'clock in the morning when my doorbell rang. The woman standing on my front porch was looking for the people who had at one time negotiated to buy our house. I explained that they had changed their mind about purchasing this property but I could very easily contact their real estate agent and find out where they had moved. When she replied, "No, it's all right, I was so upset that I just wanted to go for a long drive in the country but when I saw this place I realized I knew who bought this house so I stopped. I don't even know what I am doing here because I hardly even know those people", I remembered my prayer so I asked her to come in and have a coffee with me. She tearfully declined the offer saying, "No thank you, because I really don't know what I'm doing here and I need to go and sort out my life."

I knew exactly what she was doing there and I knew that God had set the whole thing up so I persisted, explaining that I did a lot of counseling and that I was certain that I could help her. Upon hearing this she raced by me so fast that it made me spin and then standing in the middle of my kitchen started to list the tragic and heartbreaking circumstances that were plaguing her life. She was in the middle of a divorce. Her children were on a plane heading to Winnipeg even as we spoke. Her home was going into foreclosure and she was not going to have a place to live. She didn't know what to do. She poured out her heart for hours thinking her life was over. I knew it was not!

By four o'clock in the afternoon I had convinced her that I knew someone who not only had all the answers but loved her to the point that He laid down His life for her and would help her get her life in order the moment she asked for His help. She was more than willing to pray with me and ask for that help. She left my house with a bible under one arm and a copy of the book I wrote under the other. My book is about how God has miraculously changed my life and His book is about how He was going to change hers. She also left with renewed hope in her heart and the assurance that God not only loved her, but that He was there for her any time she needed help and that this was the first day of the rest of her life and it was going to be filled with peace and joy and love and all good things because God was now at the center of it.

I feel so honored and I consider it such a privilege to be a part of God transforming someone's life like that. A life that is so very precious to Him. At the same time it is very humbling to realize what God can do with one simple prayer.

In Matthew 25 Jesus called His servants 'blessed of My Father' and stated that they were going to inherit the kingdom prepared for them from the foundation of the world because of all the righteous deeds they had performed unto Him and then He started listing them. They were perplexed and asked, *'Lord, when did we see you hungry and feed you, or thirsty and give you drink? When did we see you a stranger and take you in, or naked and clothe you? Or when did we see you sick or in prison and come to you? And the King will answer and say to them, "Assuredly, I say to you, inasmuch as you did it to one of the least of these my brethren, you did it to me".'* (NKJV)

~ 55 ~

It's really 'no big deal' for God

Lately I've noticed that so many more people are seriously worried about the economy and very anxious about their future that I have decided that I needed to comment on it in this article.

Whenever anybody shares a concern, just as Jesus told stories to illustrate His point and reveal who God is, I respond by telling a story from my own life that shows how God has supernaturally intervened in a similar situation. As I've explained in a previous article, I named my ministry Psalm 40 Ministries because the essence of Psalm 40 states that *"others will see what God has done for me, and put their trust in Him".*

Therefore I would like to tell you about the day that I was getting ready to go to preach in a church in Louisiana. I was just about ready to leave when I noticed that my outfit needed some pizzazz. Even though my skirt had these gargantuan polka dots all over it, my top was basic black on black and I thought I looked a bit too plain. I tried changing my earrings to something quite a bit larger but felt that all these various earrings were screaming so loudly that people would not hear what I was saying. So instead I tried on some lovely and very up-to-date necklaces but quickly decided that they were just too ostentatious. I am just not that flamboyant. At least not in appearance. Although, my son Mike tells me that when it comes to my personality that I am so animated that I should be a cartoon character. But we'll just leave that alone for right now. We don't need to go there.

As I stood looking at my boring ensemble I thought, "I should get one of those 'black, plastic, rope-type things' that hang around your neck and then I could hang something on it. Maybe like one of the rocks that I saw encased in silver, or something similar. Something that would add some color." I was thinking 'rocks' as in 'granite', not as in 'diamonds'.

Tucking that thought away at the back of my mind, I headed off to church praying that my message would not be as uninteresting as my appearance. I'm happy to report that I managed to hold everyone's attention and didn't catch anyone snoozing. After my message I then spent almost an hour praying for people down at the altar. Just as I finished praying for the last person, I noticed a very young man standing at the back of the church. Suddenly, I felt drawn to him like a magnet. As I made my way over to him, wanting to ask if he needed prayer, I thought, "Of course he doesn't want prayer. He's going to say 'No'. If he wanted prayer he would have come down to the alter." So I was actually shocked when he agreed to have me pray for him.

I laid my hand on his shoulder and prayed for what seemed like a couple of minutes. When I finished praying I opened my eyes to see him holding out a closed fist. He gazed at me with the most soul-searching eyes and said, "You are not going to believe this. I was in the rest room washing my face when I heard God say, 'Give this to the evangelist'." He then opened his fist and presented me with a most beautiful and very intricately crafted cross --- hanging from a 'black, plastic, rope-type thing'.

I started shaking like a leaf as tears involuntarily spurted from my eyes because of the sheer magnitude of what had just happened. Scripture after scripture raced through my mind... *"Delight thyself also in the Lord; and He shall give thee the desires of thine heart"* (Psalm 37:4) ... *"Seek ye first the kingdom of God and His righteousness and ALL these things shall be added unto you"* (Matthew 6:33)

When God shows me that He cares about a mere ornament that hangs around my neck, then I know that He cares about the 'REAL NEEDS' pertaining to my life. Whether financial, spiritual, physical or emotional. It does not matter what the economy is doing, or what's happening on the stock market, or how high the gasoline prices rise. My future is not in the hands of the world's system but my destiny is in the palm of God's hand.

Jesus assured those that worry about what they will eat or drink or wear with this scripture from Matthew chapter 6, *"Consider the lilies of the field, how they grow; they toil not, neither do they spin: And yet I say unto you, That even Solomon in all his glory was not arrayed like one of these. Wherefore, if God so clothe the grass of the field, which today is, and tomorrow is cast into the oven, shall He not much more clothe you, O ye of little faith? Therefore take no thought, saying, What shall we eat? or, What shall we drink? or, Wherewithal shall we be clothed? For after all these things do the Gentiles seek: for your heavenly Father knoweth that ye have need of all these things."*

He is still the same God that fed the children of Israel with manna from heaven. He has not changed. He can feed you.

~ 56 ~

A Truckload of Grief Destroys My Whole Week

What I'm about to tell you is like something from an Alfred Hitchcock movie, but it is absolutely true and it all happened in a period of just seven days --- my first seven days back in Venice. It reminded me of the ten plagues of Egypt, except that in my case I ended up with eleven.

At first it didn't seem too earth-shattering. My husband merely announced that our refrigerator wasn't working and we needed a new one. No, that was not going to be possible because our property taxes had just doubled and our income had not --- but not to worry, I was going to deal with that some other time because I had scads of other stuff to do.

Since it was really hot, I hurried to get some relief, thereby discovering that our air conditioner wasn't working either. Now THAT really annoyed me. I could possibly live without a refrigerator but air conditioning was vital to someone in my age category because I would get extremely overheated when it was 50 degrees, much less 80. With eyes wild with frenzy, I ran to my hubby and yelled, "Fix it! FIX IT!"

Moments later I was screaming once again. "Help! HELP ME!" while frantically waving and flailing my arms and running all over my front lawn because a swarm of bees were attacking me as I tried to raise my window awnings. How could I possibly know they had made a hive underneath? My overtaxed husband (no pun intended) merely said, "Leave it." So I did. Just left them hanging with one side down and the other half way up with pipes dangling and banging against the outside wall.

"What next, Lord?" I thought, "This is becoming overwhelming." I took a deep breath and decided I would just concentrate on cleaning and washing up six month's worth of neglect and that was when I discovered the four little piles of sawdust around the dresser in my back room. TERMITES? How can we have TERMITES? I immediately went into action, threw the dresser out the back door and then got on my hands and knees armed with a rag saturated with Clorox hoping to resolve this newest plague when I sustained such an electrical shock that I was surprised to find I was still alive.

Normally, three people have to die for me to cry (I'm exaggerating here a little now so that you'll get the idea) but this latest jolt caused me to stand there and sob these gargantuan tears (well maybe they weren't THAT big, but I was really shaken) until my laid-back-never-gets-upset-about-anything husband put his arm around me and said very calmly, "Did you know the printer's not working either?"

Well, that comment at least caused me to stop crying. Composing myself I rushed to my bedroom because I remembered seeing something unusual the night before which I didn't have the time or energy to deal with until now. I was horrified to find fuzz growing on the bottom of my night table. MOLD? WHY would mold be growing THERE? The answer soon became apparent as I discovered my headboard and the entire wall behind it very damp and actually rotting because the window above it had leaked while we were gone.

I tried to console myself by hoping that I was really still up in Canada and this week was just a bad dream.

Calling a contractor only made things worse. Not only was it going to cost $1,500.00, but he scared the heebie jeebies out of me as he proceeded to educate me on the hazards of mold and told me to close the room off completely until he removed the entire bedroom wall. Then he would have to bring in a machine to suck all the spores out of the air. He was certain that my insurance would cover this because it was actually 'water damage'.

"Ummm, no, that's not an option because I just got a notice that my insurance had elapsed. You see, I learned that the post office does not forward bulk mail, so that's the reason why I didn't get the bill."

When he replied, "Oh NO, your insurance will quadruple ...IF they reinstate you at all," I escorted him to the front door. Now totally exasperated, I said, "Well, thanks for your expertise but I have no insurance, no money and not enough credit, so I'm simply going to go into denial and go replant some flowers in my back yard to make myself feel better!"

I knew that was definitely NOT going to be a solution to my predicament but I didn't expect it to get worse. Within minutes I was screaming once AGAIN. The fox kept coming closer and closer. Even though I was threatening it with the water hose, it would not shoo. Coming to the rescue, my husband suspected it had babies close by so he shooed ME back into the house.

At this point I finally realized I needed divine intervention. (I don't know WHY it takes me so long). I began claiming the promise from Psalm 34, "MANY are the afflictions of the righteous ('righteous' meaning those that have right standing with God because they have accepted forgiveness for their sins through the sacrificial death of Jesus) but the Lord delivers him out of them ALL." I knew that God would resolve each and every situation for me. Not just 'some' of my afflictions, but ALL of them. Each and every one. And that He did, one after another. I can't wait to tell you about what happened, but it will have to be next month. Until then, begin to pray that scripture over your own needs and trust God to work it all out for YOU.

~ 57 ~

'Seek Ye First the Kingdom of God...'

This is such an appropriate day to write the conclusion to the article which I shared with you last month about that disastrous first week I experienced upon returning to Florida. You see, I've been sitting here for hours, overwhelmed, choking back tears of joy, trying to absorb the magnitude of what occurred just this morning. I marvel at the wonder of God. I am almost undone. I have such an overwhelming sense of God's presence.

Before I relate what just happened I need to tell you how God *'delivered me out of ALL my afflictions'*, according to Psalm 34:19 and how He realigned my understanding of all those events before that week was over.

The bees did not actually sting me ... they merely buzzed my hair (as I ran frantically back and forth across my front yard swatting them through the air). The fox didn't bite me ... it simply made me run for cover (all the while screaming and yelling as if I had become deranged). The electrical shock didn't kill me, even though I was soaking wet ... although it probably aged me considerably and possibly added some extra curl to my hair. The bottom line is, I was divinely protected through it ALL.

The termites did not eat the entire inside of my house but ended up being those flying bugs that attack the glue behind veneer ... and they're all gone now! The new dresser, which I happened to find the very next weekend at a garage sale, is a far better piece of furniture and only cost me $20. I was amazed that they weren't asking one hundred and fifty.

My insurance company reinstated me for only $26 more after just ONE phone call .. and everyone agrees it was an 'act of God' that they didn't take advantage and double my premium.

My hubby had the A/C fixed way before I was even close to the brink of heat exhaustion. But, he didn't have the same expertise when it came to the refrigerator so he took the palm of his hand and smacked the thing really hard and it's been cooling ever since. Then, when our friend Jack came over I mentioned that my printer wasn't working. He merely took the paper and turned it upside down saying, "These things are so sensitive that when the paper gets a little warped because of the dampness it won't feed through properly" and BINGO, just like that, the printer was fixed!

That $1,500 mold problem turned out to be the greatest miracle and became resolved right after class when the professor at my bible college asked, as he always does, "Does anyone need prayer?" I jumped out of my seat and yelled, "I do! I do! Wait until you hear about all that's happened to me this week!"

A young man named Jeremiah, whom I had never met before in my entire life, came up to me and said, "I'm a carpenter. The Lord's just laid it on my heart to help you with this mold situation and I'm not going to charge you anything whatsoever for the labor. I'll take down the entire wall and put up a brand new one. Not a problem!"

Someone else paid for the material and another friend just happened to have a 'mold-spore-sucking-machine' laying around her house that removed every last trace of the mold.

Are you amazed? I know that I was. BEYOND amazed! I can't help it. Even though God's word promises that He will provide ALL of the needs of His children, I'm still surprised EACH and EVERY time that He does.

Now I'll get back to why I was so deeply stirred this morning. It all began during this past month. As I hurried and scurried back and forth my spiritual and emotional tank would start getting pretty close empty. There is nothing that can fill me up quicker than to put on some Godly anointed music and spend time with the Lord but, there are places to go and people to see and things to do. So, I began longing and yearning for piano music that could quench this thirst while I was on the run, all day long,. I didn't want any singing, as that would distract me when working on the computer or counseling on the phone, so I specifically needed 'piano music' softly playing in the background, bathing over my spirit like 'manna' from heaven.

To satisfy this deep need, I made a mental note to stop at some garage sales and look for a CD. All the expenses that I had just incurred stopped me from running out to the store and just buying one. I did not say anything to anybody about this, not even my husband.

Well, I believe you know what's coming next. In the mail this morning was a Christmas card from my pastor and his wife. It was a little thicker than a regular card because it was actually a small booklet and inside this booklet was a CD which I have on right now, softly playing Christmas carols as I type this article.

And of course... there is no vocal... only piano!

God heard my heart's cry and then just popped it in the mail to me.

What can I add to this? God is so good! My heart is so full.

His word says that if we *'seek first the kingdom of God and His righteousness', that He'll see to everything else.'* (Matt. 6:33 KJV)

~ 58 ~

Let Me Give You God's Cell Phone Number

If you have been reading my articles for any length of time you probably remember that back in 1991 it seemed as if my life had blown up in my face. I use the word 'seemed' because I totally lost my understanding of God for more than three and one half years because of what transpired. We (my husband and I) were embezzled out of an incredible amount of money when we sold the 82 acre farm which we held as an investment. The funds from the sale of that farm were absolutely crucial. They were going to be used to eliminate the large mortgage that we owed on a third property which we had intended to turn into a shelter for abused women. By the time all the dust settled, we were left with exactly 36 cents to our name. This could not have happened at a worse moment in our lives because at that time we had two sons in university and our youngest son was about to enter Bible College.

Prior to that point in my life I had a direct line to heaven. Suddenly it seemed as if the phone had become disconnected and the line had gone dead. I could not hear from God. He seemed to be totally silent. What I didn't realize until after those three and one half pitiful years was that He was speaking loud and clear but not in the way I expected or was accustomed to. My focus was on what I had lost instead of on what the Lord was providing because He completely and totally met our needs, each and every one, on a day to day basis. Just as the Lord had sent the prophet Elijah to the Brook Cherith and sustained him there, He had a little brook prepared for me but I barely noticed because it was just a slow, steady trickle instead of a torrent like

Niagara Falls. I did not have a week's worth of shopping or a month's supply of groceries in my fridge, but God did send those ravens each and every day just as He did for Elijah.

I'm shocked now when I think back to that time that I did not see the hand of God supernaturally intervening again and again. I guess it was because I had always been very self-sufficient and accustomed to making truckloads of money. So, instead of focusing on God's miraculous provisions, I became so discombobulated that I could barely function. So much for my 'massive faith'! Since my husband was also a workaholic, the trauma of losing 25 years worth of blood, sweat and tears and having absolutely nothing to show for it caused him to start having heart attacks and his health deteriorated dramatically. His faith was in me rather than in God so when I began to live in a constant state of anxiety his world crumbled.

That life changing event and the years that followed taught me some incredible lessons and changed my life so dramatically that I intend to write a new book about the entire experience and the thousands of miracles that God enacted for us. There were literally thousands because God had to intervene MANY times a day because we had come to the end of ourselves and our own efforts. I know that story will help and encourage many people and give them hope to believe God in the midst of their own disastrous situations.

Sixteen years later, and now much older, something just as earthshaking happened again. But, THIS time I am not only older, I am MUCH WISER so I immediately ran to get a word from God and just happened to open my bible at 2 Chronicles chapter 20 where the Lord told King Jehoshaphat to stand still and see the salvation of the Lord. Then as Jehoshaphat stood and began to sing and praise the Lord, God intervened on his behalf. You really need to read this incredible story of God's faithfulness.

Since our current catastrophe is too big for us to handle I know that I will just have to 'stand' and believe that God will work it all out. So this morning I reminded my husband that when Paul and Silas were beaten and then thrown into that horrible dungeon, forced to sit in their own filth with their feet shackled, that they did not murmur or complain or panic but they started to sing praises to their God and suddenly an earthquake shook the prison so hard that the doors were thrust open and their chains fell off and the Lord delivered them supernaturally. (Acts 16) I then spent the morning singing and worshipping God instead of falling apart.

Later in the day I pondered some ideas and topics for this month's article. I had actually wrestled for an entire week on what to write. I was having some difficulty until just after supper when I sat at the computer and began typing this story to this very spot right here.... and that's when I received my confirmation from heaven. My friend Lena called from Dominica and said that God had prompted her to call and prophecy over me. Under a tremendous anointing she said that the Lord told her that I was in a fierce battle. I had been cast into the fiery furnace and the heat was being turned higher and hotter but that if I do (don't miss this...) what Paul and Silas did and sing praises to our God that He would release Warring Angels to deliver me. Then she continued (don't miss this either) that I should just 'stand still and see the salvation of the Lord' as Jehoshaphat did because God was going to fight on my behalf.

Then, she told me to get a flag and wave it as I sang. It would be a symbol that I already have the victory. Then (it just gets better) she said that the Lord specifically wanted me to read Psalm 27. When I turned to that psalm I saw a notation in the margin that said, 'see FLAG article #40 March 2002'.

That's three separate, prophetic confirmations of God's intended intervention. How's THAT for a direct line to heaven?

Many of you are in the fight of your lives and it's taking everything within you to maintain your faith in God but this article is YOUR answer from heaven and the Lord is saying to you, "Trust in me. I will see you through this problem. Don't let the devil steal your joy. Sing songs of praise! Rejoice! Then watch and see what marvelous things I will do for you!"

The perfect ending to this article is a quote from Jeremy Taylor ... "It is impossible for that man to despair who remembers that his Helper is omnipotent."

His number is 1-800-SING-PRAISES-TO-HIS-NAME

~ 59 ~

Sing in the Midst of Disaster

Last month I was pretty excited because the Lord had intervened so supernaturally regarding a pretty serious crisis that had cropped up in my life. In actuality that predicament was just the culmination of a long list of extenuating circumstances that had escalated and progressed until it became apparent that all these very grave and life-altering events were not a normal progression of circumstances but were obviously an attack orchestrated by 'the powers of darkness' that Ephesians chapter 6 talks about. I mean, it was like the powers of hell were suddenly unleashed.

They were certainly far beyond my natural ability to resolve. So, I imitated what those bold and fearless men of God in the bible did when they were powerless and I began to sing and praise the Lord. That is what King Jehoshaphat did in the Old Testament and that is what Paul and Silas did in the New until God fought the battle on their behalf and delivered them. I was more than happy to relinquish this entire mess to the One that has some serious clout, not only in heaven but also on earth.

Although I don't want to repeat myself I need to reiterate the part about how the Lord showed a friend, who lives thousands of miles away, that I was in the fiery furnace and that the fire was getting hotter and hotter. She said that God was going to send Warring Angels to deliver me from the flames that wanted to consume me and that all I needed to do was to stand in faith and trust God and to sing, and then sing some more, the same way Jehoshaphat did when he came up against insurmountable odds and the same way Paul and Silas did when they were imprisoned.

That was amazing! The fact that she mentioned these particular people from the thousands that could have been used as an example was pretty spectacular in itself, but, God used a third confirmation which was so remarkably specific that even an atheist would have to acknowledge that it was a miracle. She told me to read Psalm 27 and to get a flag and to wave it symbolically, unbeknownst to her that I had the word 'flag' written in the notation of my bible beside that very same psalm.

How much clearer could it be? It was as if God literally arrived on the scene in the midst of all the turmoil. It was really encouraging and at the same time extremely humbling to know that God was reaching down and was about to set things straight. I realized that God was going to do battle for me. I had total peace. I certainly didn't need any additional proof or further confirmation so what happened over the next two days was obviously orchestrated to build YOUR faith for the circumstances that are happening in YOUR life. Or, maybe God wants to prepare you for those things that are yet to come. Either way, I am convinced they happened so that you would know that God is aware of your situation and that He is willing to undertake for YOU.

The fact that God used David Wilkerson in these two additional confirmations, to further emphasis His solution to the dilemmas we face in our lives, is not surprising because I respect him as a prophet sent by God. Therefore the Lord has him pop up at all the strategic points in my life knowing that I will pay close attention.

The first confirmation jumped off the page and almost hit me in the face when my friend brought me a pile of mail that she had been holding for me. Tucked away in this stack was an article in which Wilkerson used King Jehoshaphat as an example, showing what he did when he faced an invasion by a massive army. As his nation trembled helplessly before this mighty force... Jehoshaphat sang! As he sang God simply had the enemy turn on itself and destroy itself.

The second confirmation, which is actually number five, was a taped message of the sermon he preached just recently warning of a sudden cataclysmic event which the Lord showed him was imminent. He believes that it is going to occur in the United States, yet the entire world is going to be affected by it. He believes that Isaiah 24 prophecies about the events of a day when everything is going to be turned upside down. It is going to be beyond man's human ability to cope with the aftermath. The world is going to be changed in one hour. He also believes that the church is going to be changed in one hour and enter her destiny. His sermon was not intended to instill fear in anyone but to show that God loves us so much that He warns us in advance.

The crux of his message though was that in the midst of all this destruction he saw that God's people will be *'singing the song of the Lord.'* They will be *'singing for the majesty of the Lord in the midst of the fire'* (Isaiah 24:14, 15 paraphrased) because the children of the Most High God do not sorrow as the world sorrows because we know that God is in control. As that old hymn so aptly declares, 'He holds the whole the world in His hands.' Therefore, we have absolutely nothing to fear.

Let me emphasize that the time to start singing is not after disaster strikes but now. Right now, begin to sing and build yourself up so that you can stand strong and bring strength and peace to those around you.

For those of you who are in the midst of your fire right now.... it is not too late to start singing because *'the eyes of the Lord run to and fro throughout the whole earth, to show HIMSELF strong in the behalf of them whose heart is perfect toward Him.'* (II Chron. 16:9 KJV)

~ 60 ~

Usually, Things Are Never What They Appear To Be

In a previous article I promised to tell you about the divine appointment which awaited me on my trip to Missouri because I wanted you to get a clearer understanding of what it means to sail smoothly through the frustrating perplexities of daily life totally confident that when we yield to the Spirit of God everything that happens to us is being orchestrated by Him so that it will ultimately work out for our good and for His glory. It is during those times when it seems like we are paddling upstream that we need to remind ourselves that God is at the helm and readily allow Him to steer the course.

My flight was delayed from the 'get-go' so I had to spend the next six hours trying to catch any flight to anywhere which would get me to my final destination. I never dreamed that the weather could be so nasty during that time of year. By the time I had to reclaim my luggage for the third time and drag it back to the departure area, where they kept reassuring me that they would get me to where I needed to be, I felt as if I had walked no less than a hundred miles. My bags, though on wheels, had become very cumbersome and a total nuisance by then. The funny thing was, even though it is not unusual for planes to be delayed and connecting flights to get messed up in bad weather, I began to sense that God had a divine purpose and that He wanted me on a particular plane at a particular time.

Eventually, I boarded a plane which was deployed to handle all the backed up traffic and was therefore mostly empty. Just as the hatch was about to close, a very flamboyant and extremely charismatic individual, who was chatting nonchalantly, but much too loudly on his cell phone, turned to the steward and said, "Have you got anything in First Class?" The steward replied quite sarcastically, as if he had encountered this ploy many times before, that First Class was booked solid but that he could have his pick of seats anywhere else on the plane.

Even though he was obviously dripping in wealth, from his full length leather coat, that was noticeably worth more than an average person's entire wardrobe, to the very expensive laptop case that was casually draped over his shoulder, everyone could tell from his telephone conversation, which was loud enough for everyone on the plane to hear, that he was accustomed to slipping into First Class free of charge.

Undaunted by the negative rebuttal and behaving like a movie star, he parked himself one row behind and across the aisle from me and began a flirtatious power struggle with the stewardess who was trying to get him to end his call. Moments later I couldn't help but overhear him negotiating with her about the price of a can of beer. She kept repeating that the price was five dollars but he kept offering her three. He explained that he didn't have a chance to get to an ATM machine so all he had on him was three bucks. Politely she kept repeating, "I'm sorry, sir, a beer costs five dollars."

Without thinking, and before I even knew what I was doing, I reached out my arm and said, "Let me throw in the two dollars!"

Now focusing her attention on me, the stewardess announced, for everyone on the entire plane to hear, "This nice lady is going to buy you a drink."

Completely alarmed at what people might be thinking, I was very quick to explain, very loudly I might add, that I don't even drink, but that I have been caught short of funds many times and could relate to his predicament."

Ignoring my feeble explanation he immediately dove into the seat opposite mine and began 'hitting' on me. Telling him repeatedly that I was NOT trying to pick him up and was on my way to see my grandchildren did not deter him in the least. His mischievous grin got even broader and his eyes became wide with expectation as he bounced around in his seat trying to find out all he could about me. Finally, determined to thwart his advances, I stammered, "I am also an ordained minister and will be preaching in Missouri this coming Sunday!"

His composure changed so dramatically that for a moment I thought the plane had stopped in midair. Suddenly the glitz and the glamour melted into a puddle of raw, broken humanity. He was desperate for something to bring meaning into his empty life. In spite of all his wealth and behind all the smoke and mirrors was a man who bore a gaping hole deep within his soul. He fired question after question at me for the next four and one half hours. I was then privileged to lead him to the saving knowledge of our Lord Jesus Christ, who alone is able to fill that void and transform his life forever.

Since we had both attracted a lot of attention and then in our exuberance talked so loudly that most everyone could hear our conversation, we had a very captive audience. I was very delighted to find out later that they felt like they had been to church.

~ 61 ~

God's Very Special Gift to You and Me

They say you can tell a lot about a person by the way he handles three things: a rainy day; lost luggage and tangled Christmas tree lights.

I have to admit that on rainy days I just want to curl up and take a nap as the sound of the rain lulls me to sleep. I think it's great that God would water my garden as I snooze. I even welcome thunderstorms. My hubby says I've slept soundly through some incredible ones. I'm not really certain what that says about me but I do hope you don't think I'm a bit lazy.

As far as lost luggage goes --- I haven't been there and I haven't done that. I hope I never do.

Now as far as tangled lights go, we need to talk. The first half of my life I did not enjoy Christmas. As far back as I can remember I was told to decorate the tree on Christmas Eve. My parents didn't help. There were no Christmas carols or warm apple cider, just extra chores and extra housework in case friends or relatives popped over. I knew there was something wrong with this picture but I wasn't too certain what that was or why it made me sad. Plus, I was always told I did it all wrong.

When I had a family of my own, I determined to make Christmas a most wonderful time of the year but found that I became overly burdened with writing cards and last minute shopping while holding down two jobs. Every year I promised myself that I would start earlier but inevitably I would get worse and worse. I would become overwhelmed because I'm not a shopper. I wish clothes would just appear in my closet rather than having to go look for them so you can imagine what looking for things for someone else does to me. Although Christmas no longer made me sad, it seemed to be all about shopping and frustration over tangled strings of lights. I was so very glad when it was all over and would not have minded in the least if Christmas was totally cancelled.

What I didn't know back then was that *'God so loved the world, that He gave His only begotten son, that whosoever believeth in Him should not perish, but have everlasting life. For God sent not His son into the world to condemn the world but that the world through Him might be saved.'* (John 3: 16, 17)

I finally discovered God. I finally discovered Jesus. I finally discovered that the tiny babe in the manger was not just an ornament under the tree but the Lord of heaven and earth. He came to show us God's everlasting love. He was God's gift to mankind, wrapped in swaddling clothes. He came knowing that He would have to lay down His life in order that you and I could be reconciled to God and thereby receive eternal life. Yet He came willing. The knowledge and then acceptance of that truth is gargantuan and has tremendous consequences.

Each year now my focus is on Emmanuel, God with us. I no longer get frustrated but celebrate the true meaning of Christmas with a heart of gratitude and a mandate to spread this glorious message to those that are still just all tangled up in Christmas tree lights. To those that haven't heard that God is WITH us and wants to live WITHIN the hearts of those that accept His glorious gift of salvation.

I wish you and your loved ones a most glorious and blessed Christmas holiday and may you carry the message of Christmas in your hearts each and every day throughout the entire new year.

~ 62 ~

A Tribute to My Dad

After a very lengthy illness my dad Nikola went to be with the Lord on May the 6th. He had been hospitalized since early December when gangrene claimed his right leg. He never regained his strength after the surgery and became weaker with each passing day so I flew to Canada on two separate occasions to spend a few weeks with him.

He was not always lucid because of all the heavy medication. The very first time I walked into his room he inquired as to who I was and I explained, with a huge lump in my throat, that I was his daughter. His eyes then searched my face very intently and then he blurted, "WHY do you look like this?" I didn't know whether to laugh or to cry and replied, "I couldn't have aged THAT much since you've last seen me!" "Oh no, no, you're beautiful," he quickly shot back, "I just don't think I've ever seen you before."

Thank God that he did know who I was MOST of the time so that we could reaffirm our love for one another. He would stroke my face lovingly as I would reminisce about the many times that he took me fishing. Since he had no sons and I was his only child he was determined to make a first class fisherman out of me. He also had me cheering for Bobby Hull, Bobby Orr and Frank Mahovlich so it's no wonder I'd rather go to a hockey game than go shopping for clothes.

I respected and admired my dad greatly. He was a giant of a man both physically and in every other way. My kids adored him also. We were shocked to find out that on top of everything else he had cancer in his bones and that it had spread to other parts of his body. It was heart breaking to see him become so weak and helpless. Even though he was very frail and in much pain from all the other complications, he never lost his will to live and although he was not able to even sit up for the last four months he would ask us daily to bring him his clothes and two strong men that could carry him to the car so he could go home. One time, after he had pulled out his feeding tube, his wife and I tried to coax him to eat on his own but he gritted his teeth and turned his head away from the spoon like a little boy would do and once again asked for his shoes (forgetting he had only one leg). We told him if he opened his mouth and chewed the food that we would bring him his shoe, and he smiled sheepishly and replied, "One shoe is not worth THAT much!" He never lost his sense of humor. He was hilarious.

He was also a very hard worker and always true to his word. He was self-taught and in spite of only a few years of schooling he could hold his own in any conversation about anything and everything. He was very well informed, very well read and he ALWAYS had an opinion. I loved the fact that he had strong convictions........EXCEPT when it came to God. Just like most people, he had his own misconceptions about God and the hereafter. Because he was raised in a communist country he could not fathom an omnipotent, omnipresent, and omniscient God. He would laugh when I talked about Jesus and then kid me that IF there was a man who walked on the water two thousand years ago then he could probably do that because he was a spaceman from another planet.

Fortunately, and because of many prayers offered up on his behalf, he did not remain in darkness. After my mother died he met a precious lady who was committed to God. She transformed his life and very shortly after he then allowed the Lord to transform him. He continually kept telling everyone that life was 'never better than this' and that he wished that he was younger so that he could enjoy it longer. In the hospital I kept reminding him that the best was yet to come because God said in 1 Cor. 2:9 "Eye hath not seen, nor ear heard, neither have entered into the heart of man, the things which God hath prepared for them that love Him." (KJV) It is the one thing that brings me comfort and lessens my grief plus the assurance that my dad is beholding the face of God and that one day in the not too distant future we will be reunited around the throne of God.

Until then, there will be a gaping hole in my life and in my heart but I will not dread any upcoming Father's Days because I know that both my Heavenly Father and my earthly dad are looking down from above, assuring me of their love.

My other reason for writing this article is to encourage everyone on this upcoming Father's Day to reach out to the Lord who longs to be known as "Abba Father" which translated means 'Daddy', implying that He wants a close, intimate relationship with His children.

He will become your Father and adopt you into the Family of God the moment you turn to the Lord Jesus Christ in repentance and receive Him as your Savior, trusting in Him alone to save you. You will then truly experience the unfathomable depth and revelation of His grace and love.

~ 63 ~

Jesus Obtained Reconciliation

Between God and His Creation

The one question incredulous people ask over and over again is, "If there is a God, why does He allow sickness and disease? Why does He allow tragedy to strike good, honest, decent people?" The mere thought that there would be a God who would orchestrate wars and inflict pain and suffering on mankind causes them to come to the conclusion that there must not be a God.

The answer is very simple --- there most definitely is a God and He does none of the above. He does not orchestrate sickness or disease. He is not the author of misery. God's intent was the Garden of Eden. His plan was that mankind, whom He created in the image of Himself, would reflect His glory and would live in Paradise totally free from death and decay and free from any and all form of evil or destruction.

I'm certain that you are all familiar with the story of Adam and Eve but I need to point out that it was way back there that 'man blew it' but he has been blaming God ever since. Adam and Eve could walk and talk with God in the cool of the day. They were created to have intimate fellowship with God. The only stipulation was that they NOT eat of the 'Tree of the Knowledge of Good and Evil.' God said that if they did, they would die.

He did not specify that they would die immediately but by disobeying God's explicit command they opened the door to death and disease and all the other afflictions that have overtaken mankind ever since. The entire planet has been reaping the consequences of their behavior. Romans 8:22 says, *"The whole creation groaneth and travaileth in pain together until now."*

That was the bad news. The good news is that God had a plan from the beginning of time to remove the barrier created by sin which was erected between Him and His creation. That plan was to send Jesus to be a propitiation for our sinful fallen state. Jesus gave His life as a ransom for many. He became the sinless substitute that causes us to be reconciled with God. Accepting Christ and His righteousness places us in right standing with God and it thankfully procures our forgiveness.

Sin separated us from God and brought death through Adam but if we come to God by faith in Jesus Christ we receive forgiveness and His gift of eternal life. Because Jesus conquered sin and death and rose on the third day, we are made alive in Him. We are adopted into the family of God. He becomes our heavenly Father. We become heirs of the King of Kings and the Lord of Lords.

Therefore, just as a human parent wants the best for his kids, our Father in heaven provides every good and perfect gift: love, joy, peace, healing and provision for our daily living. Jesus says in John 10:10, *"I am come that you might have life, and that you might have it more abundantly."* And again in 3rd John 1:2, *"Beloved, I wish above all things that thou mayest prosper and be in health even as thy soul prospereth."*

This is still not the end of the story. He also says that He has gone to prepare a place for us, a mansion in heaven where the streets are paved with gold and where He will wipe away our tears.

An even more exciting promise is, *"Eye hath not seen, nor ear heard, neither have entered into the heart of man, the things which God hath prepared for those that love Him."*

My prayer is that you will open your heart and ask the Lord Most High to become your Savior so that He can elevate you to be seated in Him at the right hand of God the Father, now and for all eternity.